SPLINTERED INNOC

AN INTUITIVE APPROACH TO TREAT

Peter Heinl

SPLINTERED INNOCENCE

AN INTUITIVE APPROACH TO TREATING WAR TRAUMA

THINKAEON

www.thinkclinic.com

drpheinl@btinternet.com

Twitter: @DrPeterHeinl und @Thinkclinic

Facebook: www.facebook.com/peter.thinkclinic

LinkedIn: Peter Heinl

Xing: Peter Heinl

Layout: uwe kohlhammer

Illustrations: Matheus Heinl

Cover design: Peter Heinl

First published 2001 by Brunner-Routledge

27 Church Road, Hove, East Sussex, BN3 2FA

Simultaneously published in the USA and Canada

by Taylor & Francis Inc.

29 West 35th Street, New York, NY 10001

Brunner-Routledge is an imprint of the Taylor & Francis Group

© 2001 Peter Heinl

In remembrance of the members of my generation
whose innocent lives were taken in their childhoods
by a senseless worldwide war

CONTENT

CHAPTER 3
COMPLEXITIES, CONNECTIONS AND UNCONSCIOUS CONSTRUCTS

CHAPTER 4
RECOGNISING PATTERNS

CHAPTER 5
UNCOVERING (POST-)WAR TRAUMA

CHAPTER 6
TO SEE OR NOT TO SEE ... THE UNCONSCIOUS. THE ROLE OF INTUITION

CHAPTER 7
BETWEEN DESPAIR AND HOPE.

PREFACE

In the new millennium, global peace remains elusive and the demon of war as present, as ever. The 'War on Terrorism', the wars and convulsions of civil strife in Afghanistan and Iraq, the devastating civil war that pushed Syria into an abyss of destruction causing millions of refugees to flee their native country, the bloody conflict affecting Ukraine and ominously threatening regional security are just some examples of wars and terrifying mayhem that have ravaged parts of the globe. They often ruthlessly and brutally overstep the rules laid out by military conventions, while leaving a trail of destruction, misery, losses, death, heartbreaking tragedies and countless shattered and maimed lives of innocent civilians, children, women, sick and old people.

Against this background *Splintered Innocence*, first published in 2001, has lost none of its relevance. The observations and conclusions regarding the dimension and the spectrum of the long-term psychological trauma unleashed on a whole generation of children by the horrifying destructive forces of the Second World War remain as true today as they were then and possibly more so. The transmission of war-induced trauma on subsequent generations needs to be much more widely recognised and become an integral part of mental health thinking. There is also an urgent need to recognise trauma lodged in the unconscious that have remained undiagnosed while exercising their damaging influence over the lives of people and their offspring.

From a psychological perspective, the Second World War is not a matter of history. Its dark and destructive legacy, however deeply buried, remains alive in the minds of millions of people across the planet whether they witnessed this horrific war or are descendants of war victims. Although *Splintered Innocence* deals primarily with trauma induced by the Second World War and its long-term repercussions – and some cases of trauma due to the First World War – it also provides a blueprint for dealing with the traumatic psychological landscape of wars and armed conflicts that have ravaged many countries in many parts of the globe over the last seventy years, some of those savage conflicts meting out for decades nothing but blood, tears, endless misery and countless deaths.

It is my hope that the Thinkaeon edition of *Splintered Innocence* continues to be a helpful if not invaluable guide to a whole range of professionals, namely, psychiatrists, psychotherapists and family therapists, psychologists, medical specialists with a special interest in psychological and psychosomatic conditions, counsellors and all those professionals who are working with and caring for war-wounded victims. I very much hope, too, that *Splintered Innocence* may help sufferers to recognise whether a war-induced cause may be at the root of their psychological problems and ailments, and help to point to ways to improve or overcome their predicaments. I also hope that *Splintered Innocence* will raise the awareness of the terrible price wars exact from human beings and that it is worth fighting for peace. Despite thousands of wars having been fought in the history of mankind, and despite thousands of history books and studies having been written about wars, the topic of the long-term psychological effects of war on human beings, and children in particular, is a field in great and urgent, if not desperate, need of receiving the attention it deserves.

It is a very great pleasure to thank Keith Conlon for his stimulating suggestions and for having advised me on some issues relating to a particular phenomenon of the English language that has no meaning on its own while exercising a subtle influence over the meaning of sentences by its presence or absence, namely, commas. It is with enormous pleasure that I like to thank Suzie Grogan, the author of the splendidly written, masterful account *Shell Shocked Britain: The First World War's Legacy for Britain's Mental Health* for her passionate interest in the topic of war and for her advice and guidance on complex subtleties of the English language. And I am delighted to thank Uwe Kohlhammer for devoting, not for the first time, his admirable patience, imaginative skills and craftsmanship towards the metamorphosis of a digital file into a book that, while dealing with the demon of war, will, hopefully, assist to promote and strengthen the cause of peace.

January 2015   Peter Heinl

PREFACE
TO THE FIRST EDITION 2001

When I published a smaller version of this book in the spring of 1994 for a German readership, history had moved on since the end of the Second World War and, indeed, moved in order to escape its own legacy. Time had covered memories like snow settling on a landscape blurring out its rougher edges. In most European countries, the traces of the Second World War had been erased. It would have been difficult, for instance, to find the traces of war in what used to be former West Germany. Bullet marks in buildings had been filled, collapsed ceilings rebuilt and façades restored. The sight of blackened ruins had retreated between the pages of history books as if they had never existed in reality. White arrows indicating the nearest air raid shelters had been painted over. Tank wrecks and the remains of shot-down aeroplanes had long been removed. Bridges crossed the rivers again, as if there had never been a time when their twisted and tormented arcs had pointed sharply upwards, as if they were pleading with the skies to end the apocalypse of war.

An observer would have noted that most passers-by wore clothes of sufficient quality to protect them against the cold. Frostbitten or starving people were unlikely to cross one's path in this part of the western hemisphere, where the flames of war had been ignited more than half a century ago. Nowhere to be seen were those people whose gazes reflected the horror of events that they had witnessed and who were unable to convey in words what they had seen. An astute observer would not have taken long to realise that there was hardly a trace left of the Second World War. Ashes and the shifting sands of time had covered the 'footprints' of war. Therefore it appeared a less than burning issue to look into the effects of childhood war trauma and their repercussions throughout adult life.

Observational curiosity and unexpected encounters, however, alerted me to the psychological sequelae of war trauma in childhood. As a psychiatrist, psychotherapist and family therapist, I was familiar with a wide spectrum of mental conditions, diagnostic concepts and treatment approaches. Yet, at first, I was unprepared for the drama of suffering that was unfolding in front of me and staring at me from the faces, eyes and gestures of adults who were in my care.

As I began to recognise these phenomena, I detected a common thread in that these patients had histories of childhood war trauma. Despite the progress of time – and against the tide of forgetting – childhood war trauma, which had been buried for decades, suddenly surfaced, entering the light of consciousness with an immediacy as if these traumas had occurred only yesterday. This not only referred to adults who relived the way the war had afflicted their childhood lives. It was also evident amongst adults born after the end of the conflict, but whose parents had been caught between the merciless millstones of war.

Overcoming initial scepticism, I became gradually aware that what I had perceived represented the tip of an iceberg of suffering that had been moved out of sight of the wider public consciousness. This suffering was particularly heartrending as it had affected individuals during their early stage of development. In many cases the suffering had remained unconscious, unresolved and unrecognised because the topic of war-related trauma encountered in childhood had, certainly in Germany, remained largely unattended by psychotherapists, psychiatrists, researchers and, indeed, the mental health field as a whole.

Gradually, I was able to discern certain patterns and to find a language for their description which, I hope, does justice to the enormous complexity of the topic, while at the same time conveying the sheer madness of the suffering inflicted. In the light of this aim, I have tried to present the psychological manifestations of war-related trauma in adults, and the transmission of the suffering from one generation to the next.

I hope this book will make a contribution to the theory, diagnosis and treatment of war-related trauma in childhood, and highlight the need for special treatment centres because, sadly, there is no end in sight to wars on this planet.

As a result, new victims are accumulating daily. The childhood sufferers of today will be the suffering adults of tomorrow while peace stands by helplessly.

There is one conclusion that can be drawn firmly with respect to children in wartime, be it victory or defeat: children tend to be the great losers overlooked by history.

I am grateful that I have been offered the opportunity to see this book appear in the English language where its message can be spread beyond the German-speaking countries.

It has been very much on my mind to raise the awareness on a worldwide level and to expose the still large extent of unrecognised suffering among adults, which continues to overshadow their lives half a century after the end of the Second World War. It has been my aim to describe my findings in a way that can be easily understood by individuals whose lives have been affected by the demonic script of war. As far as the English version of my book is concerned, I have added three case reports, namely 'The Silver Necklace', 'The Enigma of the Desert' and 'A Journey into the Abyss of Consciousness: The Story of a Child Witness,' as they provide further illustrations of the issues involved.

In addition, the second part of the original German version has been expanded. I have enlarged Chapter 6 'To see or not to See ... the Unconscious. The Role of Intuition', in order to provide a fuller description of my approach to working through intuitive perception and thinking. I hope this will accommodate the reader who is interested in conceptual issues. I hope, too, that the clarification of conceptual issues will help to fuel an unbiased debate about the place of intuition in psychotherapy. Finally I hope that the account will show that we may see more with our eyes than we commonly think.

Books are rarely the result of just one individual. This book could not have been written without the generous trust shown to me by a great number of people during the course of my work. To them I express my gratitude. There are also a number of people to whom I would like to thank for their interest, support and encouragement in my work. I would like to thank my brother, Dr T. Heinl, for offering me the opportunity to conduct seminars at his beautiful country place, the Soonwald Schlösschen in the Hunsrück in Germany, and to my late mother, Dr H. Heinl, a pioneer in orthopaedic psychosomatics, for her admirable organisational work in the background. I would also like to thank Mrs B. Heller for organising the first conference of its kind on childhood war trauma in Germany in autumn 1999 at the Evangelische Akademie in Hofgeismar. I am grateful to Mrs U. Geiss for showing the same degree of encouragement she showed when I wrote the German version of this book, and to Mrs B. Motzki and to Mr B. C. Motzki for their perceptive and inspiring words of encouragement. It is only in hours of need that an author begins to realise the vital role a computer can play, and I am therefore very grateful to Mr D. Billy for having given me crucial lessons about computing; I am also grateful to him, Mr S. Patel and Mr J. Woodruff of Mygate for having provided generous support. I wish to thank Dr P. Smith for allowing me to quote from his doctoral thesis, and I very much appreciate the efficient help of Mr C. Hölting, Dipl. Psych., with the literature search. I shall always feel indebted to Dr S. Kay and to Dr P. D. White, London, for their encouragement.

It is a great pleasure to thank Mrs B. Green JP, London; Dr A. Grounds, Lecturer in Forensic Psychiatry, Institute of Criminology, University of Cambridge; Mrs H. Hanks, Consultant Clinical Psychologist at St. James's University Hospital, Leeds; and Mr C. Hölting, Dipl. Psych., Dresden, for having taken the time and care to read the manuscript and to let me have their comments and views. Of course, the final responsibility rests with me, but I feel privileged and enriched having received their perception of the manuscript. I would also like to thank Mrs B. Green JP for kindly providing translations of several German and French quotations.

I am most grateful to Mrs R. Bottini, São Paulo, for negotiating the book rights, for her steady hand, professional acumen and farsightedness. I am delighted to thank Mrs K. Hawes, Senior Editor at Routledge, for her vivid interest, open-mindedness and for the crucial role she played and care she took regarding the project. I would also like to thank her and her colleagues Mrs J. Foreshaw, Mr D. Hammond, Ms K. Susser and to all those at Routledge and Psychology Press who have worked diligently behind the scenes for their spirited efforts to bring the project to fruition.

My very special thanks are due to my daughter Sophia for her enthusiasm for the project, her flair in guiding me through the labyrinth of the English language, and for her help with corrections. She provided the title for this book and her poem *'Splintered Innocence'* at the end. I also wish to thank my son Matheus for his keenness to produce the illustrations. I thank both for their concern that young people should know about wars in order to understand one simple truth: that there would be much less suffering without armed conflicts and that the world would be a more beautiful planet.

Peter Heinl

CHAPTER 1

VICTIMS WITHOUT WORDS.
THE SHADOWS OF WAR ON ADULT FACES

Vor Pest, Hunger und Krieg
bewahre uns, oh Herr

Inschrift auf einem Wegkreuz, errichtet im Kriegsjahr 1918
nahe der Ortschaft Zornheim

Save us, oh Lord, from the plague, hunger and war

Inscription on a wayside cross erected in 1918
near the village of Zornheim, Germany

THE DISTANT THUNDER OF HISTORY

In the early 1980s the psychiatric team of one of London's teaching hospitals expected the arrival of a new patient, a young woman, with a distinct feeling of apprehension. Having originally been admitted for investigation of a suspected epileptic illness to another hospital, her transfer became a matter of urgency when she showed signs of suicidal behaviour. The seriousness of the suicidal impulses was such that the various clinical tests envisaged to examine the epilepsy had to be abandoned in order to transfer her to a special psychiatric unit without further delay.

The first impression of a seemingly shy and inconspicuous young woman seemed at odds with the anxieties preceding her arrival. Before long, however, the team and I were to know better. Her suicidal impulses were such that she did not hesitate to inflict harm on herself, even with a plastic spoon. There was little alternative but to take the decision to keep her under close and round-the-clock observation.

It was clearly of importance to gain insight into what drove this young woman to resort to such self-destructive behaviour, and it was important to do so without losing much time. The diagnostic possibility of an epileptic illness was quickly disproved. Similarly, suggestions of an eating disorder were not confirmed. Asking the young woman about her life and possible traumatic events in her biographical background did not provide any clues to explain her suicidal tendencies. Her replies were sparse, and the little information she volunteered did not shed light on an understanding of her behavioural pattern. Screening through past medical records proved fruitless. Again and again the question arose as to the cause of the suicidal impulses, which were in stark contrast to her otherwise unassuming and quiet composure. As time passed by, her predicament seemed increasingly elusive and mysterious.

Having exhausted other potential sources of information, I decided to invite the young woman's parents for an interview. Fascinated by the approach of family therapy, which aims at viewing mental health issues in individuals against the background of disturbed relationships between family members, I was pursuing the question as to whether the young woman's suicidal displays might be attributed to as yet unrecognised influences, operating in her family and throwing their dark shadows over this young woman's path into adulthood.

In the interview, I found myself facing a courteous middle-aged couple. Their daughter, the patient, had been invited to participate. The patient appeared calmer than usual and even quite relaxed. No significant features emerged from discussions about the life of her father, whose virtuoso performance of English charm and detachment was memorable. He would have been the kind of person with whom I would have liked to chat about all sorts of things, had it not been my brief to try to detect a link between possible traumatic events in his life, which, in turn, may have thrown their black veil around his daughter's existence. However, neither conscious nor intuitive clues emerged to bring me closer towards shedding light on the mystery of this young woman's behaviour.

I emphasise the term 'intuitive'. Even though the practice of psychiatry and psychotherapy is guided by scientific principles, there is always scope to use one's 'sixth sense', in order to find hypotheses or even solutions to problems which are not immediately accessible to logical enquiry. I then turned my attention to the patient's mother. I was soon to discover that she was not of English, but of German-Czech descent. Having some knowledge of the history of this particular region, in the heart of Europe with its glories and its abysses, I became curious as to her biographical background. I began by asking her questions about her life which had started in the years before the onset of the Second World War, in what was then Czechoslovakia. It was her family's bicultural German-Czech descent which caused them first to suffer discrimination at the hands of the German administration during the German occupation of the Czech lands from 1938 – 1945. Nevertheless, three of her brothers were called up into the German army and were to perish during the war.

After the resurrection of the Czechoslovak Republic in the spring of 1945, the family was unfortunate enough to be on the wrong side of history again, this time suffering at the hands of the Czech authorities. Several surviving members of her family, including herself, one of her sisters and her parents (i.e. the patient's maternal grandparents) were arrested by the Czech police.

So vivid was the account she gave me that it seemed as if time had turned back and one could hear the noises of the police officials storming up the staircase, forcing their way into the spacious apartment and then, a short while later, leaving behind the eerie silence of empty rooms and wallpaper splashed with blood. All the family members were thrown into a camp, where her father perished and her sister succumbed to madness.

More than once her tears replaced words to describe what had happened in those dark hours of European history. The sequence of senseless events seemed as close now as it had been back then. So profound was her mental anguish that her body turned and twisted in the timeless agony of pain. I wondered whether it was right to let the mother return home, as it perhaps seemed advisable to admit the mother to the ward in place of her daughter who appeared relieved and listened calmly and attentively while the drama of the life of her mother unfolded.

This memorable encounter proved a turning point for the patient. From now on, there was a noticeable improvement in her mental condition. A few months later, she had recovered to the extent that it was possible to discharge her from hospital.

It seemed that a link had been established between the mysterious suffering of the daughter and the predicament which had afflicted her mother's life. Although I had little understanding as to the causal nature of this link it made sense in the light of family therapy thinking whereby an individual's mental suffering is shaped by issues and forces operating within the family system.

There was, however, another dimension which had been revealed: the demonic horror of war. At the same time, I did not really seem able to grasp the true dimension of what I had witnessed and to relate it to this young lady and her mother. Somehow, in the 'real world' of the present, the years of the Second World War appeared to have long since faded away into the pages of history books.

THE SILENCE OF THE GUITAR

Fascinated by the way in which families create their own 'culture', sets of rules and forms of psychological organisation, I wanted to learn how family dynamics influence and shape the lives of their individual members over generations. I therefore decided to complete a course in family therapy. Later, I led seminars to explore these issues in groups. In one of these seminars, which took place in Germany in the early 1980s and which lasted five days, I explored the family history of the seminar participants by studying the drawings each of them had made of their three generational family trees or geneograms.

Entering the seminar room, on the third day, in the afternoon after a break, I found it empty, apart from one female participant who sat alone in a corner playing the guitar. After the other participants joined in, she stopped playing, putting the guitar aside. When the seminar was ready to resume, she indicated her wish to talk about her family and what had happened to them.

Trying to make a start she soon hesitated, and then became silent. The words seemed to have fallen from her hands, like marbles rolling further and further away. A motionless silence was all that remained. From looking at the expression in her eyes a surge of anxiety and horror appeared to have overwhelmed her. I felt that something terrible must have befallen her. However, rather than breaking the silence, I felt that she needed time for the words to return to her.

There was a long wait, until she said she was unable to talk about what had happened to her. She was only able to say that intense inner images had filled her mind. However, she was unable to find words for those images which she described as 'films', whose sheer terror went beyond words. I listened without saying anything. After a while I placed the guitar back into her hands. Then she played some melodies, as if to express something through sounds where words had failed.

During the following years, she attended a series of similar seminars. On each occasion she discovered new fragments of language which helped her to describe the story of her family, of her own life and of events as they had taken place. The account which gradually and painfully emerged is by no means unique. In many ways it can be seen as an icon for the lives of many members of her generation.

She was born in 1940 in East Prussia, which was then still part of Germany. Towards the end of the Second World War, when she was less then five years old, she was raped by soldiers of the advancing Soviet army. Her father, she said, might have protected her, had he not been already reported missing while in action, but he never returned. A short while later her grandfather was shot before her eyes. His dying body collapsed over her, forcing her child's body and its innocent spirit to feel the weight of death.

She became seriously physically ill. The superhuman efforts of her mother helped her to survive her illness, but one of her sisters succumbed to the infectious disease. Not much later she and her remaining family were forced to leave their homeland and had to flee. The ensuing chaos separated her and her younger brother from her mother and sister. She and her brother were small children of hardly primary school age and both were now left to their fate, drifting across a war-torn world which, long since, the gods seemed to have turned a blind eye to.

During a train journey, her brother died in the icy cold. His stiff frozen corpse was thrown out of the train window as they crossed a bridge over a river. There was no grave, no prayer and no memory as to where this happened. The way his short life ended was all that would be imprinted in her memory for the rest of her life.

Half a year later, she arrived in the West in the relatively safe area of the former American occupied zone, where she was reunited with her mother. Having lost more than half her family in the abyss of the war her mother was struck down by a long and serious mental breakdown. She, the lady with the guitar, was now forced to work in a church institution where no human warmth nor any signs of mercy were shown to her.

However, she survived through all the turmoil. Decades later she found, at last, the language to give an account of what had happened to her. She lived her life on her own and had not formed any relationships, as the wounds of rape had been too enduring to heal. Some years after the first seminar she received an unexpected present from a relative. This was a photograph of her younger brother who had died as a little boy. Again and again, she looked at the photograph, surprised, overwhelmed, even somewhat perplexed as she had lost the conscious recollection of what her brother had looked like during his brief childhood.

Whatever I may have read in history books, she, the lady with her guitar, an unassuming manner and moving words, showed me that war is more than just a sequence of events and facts. War comprises, too, whatever has been imprinted into the sensitive minds and souls of the children, with letters too dark to fade in a lifetime.

For years it had seemed to me that war was an issue of the past and of more concern to historians than to mental health professionals. This quiet woman, however, whom I had never heard utter a word of bitterness about her war-torn life, helped to open my eyes to the real psychological dimensions of war.

ANGST.
THE GRIMACE OF WAR

Conducting seminars on family issues, along the lines I have outlined, had become a significant component of my professional work by the mid-1980s. Generally speaking, the families' ability to provide a caring, nourishing and secure environment for the growth of the next generation crucially depended on a variety of conditions such as clarity of the family structure, well-defined boundaries, clear communicative patterns, an atmosphere of mutual respect and perception and, indeed, the presence of that most precious of human qualities, the capacity for love. The more those conditions were lacking, however, the more likely it was that individual family members were left to suffer in loneliness and in mental and physical distress.

However, even operating within this general framework of understanding did not provide a means of recognising and solving problems. I could never predict at the outset what issues would move into the foreground. Often I was as surprised as the seminar participants themselves at the puzzles and dramas unfolding before our eyes. In particular, this proved to be the case when I was asked to facilitate access to early childhood events in cases where conscious awareness had been lost.

In one such seminar, a female participant asked me to assist her in opening the gate of memory to her early childhood experiences, to which she had no conscious access. These experiences had occurred before she was five years old and had taken place during the war and its aftermath. All she knew was the fact that she had been born to a family belonging to a German minority in a sizeable town in an East European country. In 1945, then aged three, she had been forced to flee, together with her mother, in order to seek refuge in the

West. She emphasised that she did not possess any recollection of her flight or associated events.

I soon realised that it was pointless to persist with questioning in order to try to obtain further information about this early period of her life, as it lay hidden outside the reach of her conscious grasp. Finding myself in a kind of void of ignorance, there was nothing which would have provided me with a clue as to how to proceed in order to fulfil her request. All I observed at this stage was that the seminar participant appeared anxious and tense, but this told me little about what might have happened during her childhood.

Much to my regret, I had to tell her that I did not know what had happened to her, because I had not witnessed the events which she had lived through. Neither logical thinking nor common sense could help me to find out what she had experienced at the time and how this might have affected her. Of course, there was ample scope for speculating about what she might possibly have experienced. This, however, would have missed the point of her request as she had asked for conscious insight and recognition into what she had experienced and not into what she might have experienced.

There is always scope for hope, but this situation looked less than promising. The only way I could possibly hope to shed some light on this obscure issue was to try an approach which I had been developing since the early 1980s. This involved the application of intuitive perception and the use of objects. Although this did not appear to represent a systematic approach, nor a rationally designed method in the conventional sense, I had observed that it could provide the basis for often unexpected, surprising and accurate insights into the patterns of early life events and trauma. Guided by intuitive perceptions, which would form themselves in deeper layers of my consciousness, I would choose various objects in order to construct a composition of objects, or object sculpt, in the space of the seminar room.

Despite the atmosphere in the room I found myself in a cheerful and relaxed mood. I decided to proceed along the lines of an object sculpt. As usual, no strategic plan had so far formed in my mind. I was entirely in the dark as to how to find a solution to the problem before me. Having no plan, I should have had no reason to be in cheerful mood, but, possibly, a sense of freedom inspired me as there was seemingly little to lose and much to be gained from developing a creative context in which to work. Maybe I was simply being carried away by pursuing my seemingly playful work with objects, not much different from a child that indulges in playing while forgetting the world around. Even if my actions appeared to be against the laws of reason, a pervading sense of confidence and certainty inspired and guided me, a sense that had always accompanied me in the past in this kind of work with objects designed to explore early life experiences.

I had observed that, whenever such arrangements of objects had been completed, the composition of objects had, in their silent language, conveyed a meaning which established new links of understanding between current states of consciousness and events that had occurred in childhood.

I started by placing a black plastic chair into the centre of the seminar room, without making any comments. Indeed, how could I have said anything useful as I was in the dark as to my own actions and where they were going to take me? Funny comments came to my mind and I proceeded by attaching various objects to the chair, either with sticky tape or by hanging them over the back of the chair. Again, I can only emphasise that I did not think about the deeper meaning while I grasped the objects. Their choice was left to my hands and it was for them to decide where the objects would be placed. My hands seemed guided by these impulses emerging from deeper layers of consciousness within me.

Two candles, a red rose, a pencil, a butterfly made from paper, an egg in a glass, another second egg swinging from the chair, a dry flower and finally a pullover thrown across the chair in a haphazard way, were amongst the objects which I used in the pursuit of this 'work'.

When I finished, I appeared to have succeeded in creating a surrealistic composition, which seemed at odds with the request of the seminar participant to explore her early life. Indeed, the absurdity of what I had created would have tempted a detached observer to question the rationale of my 'work' – and possibly that of my mind, too! It seemed impossible to detect any profound meaning in what I was trying to demonstrate.

Nevertheless, having completed my 'work' I felt satisfied and filled with a sense of achievement. Even when stepping back to look at my 'work' for a while I did not feel the need to talk to anybody as my creation spoke for itself.

Quite unexpectedly, however, a further strange sensation emerged in my mind. At first I was not sure whether this was a real sensation because it had a very distant, even alien quality. The stronger it became in intensity, the more it contrasted with the cheerful spirit which had been my state of mind so far. And the stronger it grew, the nearer it seemed to come towards me. Approaching me now with a force beyond my control, it propelled itself with vehemence into my consciousness, urging me to do something which had not crossed my mind at all; namely, to destroy the 'work' with the objects I had just created.

This was very perplexing. Why should I destroy something which I had enjoyed composing and which, however ridiculous it might have appeared, radiated such an air of innocent tranquillity? Surprised and confused by this sudden and inexplicable change in the landscape of my inner perceptions, I hesitated to give in to this perplexing impulse because I felt no desire to indulge in senseless destruction.

As the impulse advanced relentlessly, I finally surrendered by giving in to it. Reluctantly, I kicked the chair with my foot until it fell over. The objects smashed to the ground. Some were crushed under the weight of the chair, others splintered into fragments, as if a violent storm had raged across a peaceful and idyllic scene.

Out of the blue, and for reasons which defied rational comprehension, a dramatic change had taken place which had transformed the scene beyond recognition. The pullover lay on the floor, with its distorted contours reminiscent of a dead person lying amidst a collection of wrecked objects. A dream of fun and quiet tranquillity had been wrecked in utter destruction.

I was still at a loss to understand what had happened, and why I had done it, when the woman rose from her seat. Without saying a word, she had followed the sequence of events right up to its crescendo. Now she stepped forward to the centre of the seminar room, where she stood in an eerie silence. She was motionless and her eyes were fixed on the scenario of destruction displayed in front of her. After a while, she started to cry until her whole body shook, as if overcome by convulsions of pain that had been locked away for endless years.

It took some time for her to calm down. Eventually, she recounted that, for the first time in her life, images of the flight from her country of origin had flooded back into her mind. She and her mother had been amongst a group of fleeing refuges who had come under attack from fighter planes. Both of them only survived the machine gun fire by throwing themselves into a ditch. After the attack, the road to freedom had been transformed into a road to death, covered with human corpses and dead horses.

In the end, she described a sense of relief. She said how important it had been for her consciously to become aware of her early traumatic encounter with war. As far as I was concerned, the outcome of this piece of work with objects stimulated and challenged my thinking. It was evident that a traumatic event, of which I had possessed no prior factual knowledge, had been brought into the sphere of consciousness. The traumatic event had occurred in childhood and had remained buried in the unconscious for decades.

Yet my conclusion suggested that, despite its unconscious quality, the trauma must have been transmitted through some channels of communication. Otherwise I would not have been able to perceive a trauma of this kind nor to help this woman to recover access to the memory of the traumatic episode which had prevailed for so long within the depths of her unconscious.

However, I lacked a conceptual framework for understanding how I had perceived the trauma the woman had experienced. It seemed plausible to attribute my discovery of this war trauma to intuition, although such a notion was purely descriptive and did not provide an explanation regarding the workings of the perceptive and thinking processes involved.

Nevertheless, there was one aspect which had by now become clear to me. Even though about four decades had passed since the end of the Second World War, childhood war trauma appeared to have remained alive, however much the memories may have been pushed or retreated into the catacombs of the unconscious. As I had come to recognise, they were open to perception, even though the question as to how this occurred was unanswered and my way of 'working' was at variance with convention.

Relying on the evidence I had gathered, the time appeared to have come for me to detach myself from the constraints of conventional thinking in order to move forward. If until then scepticism may have prevailed within me regarding the intuitive way in which I appeared to have 'picked up' subtle cues, I was now becoming keen to observe and to record the processes taking place in my own mind when carrying out such explorative work. With hindsight, it was probably fortunate that I did not know how long it would take before deeper insights would emerge.

A SPELL OF DIZZINESS

A few years later, in 1990, a colleague referred a male patient to me, requesting an assessment for psychotherapeutic treatment. While on holiday, the patient had suffered a spell of dizziness. Neurological investigation, including a brain scan, had excluded an organic lesion as a cause of the episode. It was therefore concluded that the attack of dizziness was due to a psychological cause, and the referral letter suggested that the dizziness had to be understood as the result of an unresolved, unconscious conflict between the patient and his parents. However, I had a sense of dissatisfaction with the reasoning developed in the letter.

I had been impressed with the lucid presentation of the argument. However, this did not alter the fact that I found myself left with a strange feeling of being unconvinced, which had emerged from nowhere. I was unable to substantiate this with any counterargument. Since I had not even seen the patient, I had no choice but to accept the conflict between the argument elaborated in the letter and my strange inner response to it. So, I filed the letter in the case notes and continued with my work schedule.

A few days later, the patient arrived for his first appointment. A tall and friendly looking man stood in front of me, greeting me with a handshake, as is the custom in Germany. I looked at him as I was greeting him and there was nothing to observe apart from, perhaps, the fact that the size of his head appeared to me to be slightly too large compared to the rest of his body. Also a distant sadness echoed through his eyes.

These were, however, little more than fleeting impressions and we walked into my office where the patient took his seat opposite me. My task now was to begin the clinical interview by recording his personal data. I therefore began by asking him for his full name, as well as where he was born and his date of birth.

However, as soon as he told me his date of birth in the autumn of 1945, my mind bypassed the sequential process of asking interview questions and I found myself referring to the scarcity of food available at the time.

The patient did not disagree with what I said, but he clearly remembered that American soldiers had given him pieces of chocolate. Thus, in his view, there had been no lack of food. Having allowed my mind to interrupt the interview proceedings, I now redoubled my efforts to take a full clinical history by recording a detailed account of the patient's biographical and family history. Hopefully, this would provide valuable information and pointers to hypotheses to explain the psychological origin of his recent predicament.

It did not take long before I experienced an unexpected sensation which, strangely enough, suggested I should put my paper and the case records aside. I felt compelled to get up from my chair, to look for some baby food, and to find a bib to put round the patient's neck in order to start feeding him – as if the big man sitting in front of me had been suddenly and magically transformed into a tiny, hungry baby. It appeared that part of my thought processes had shaken off the leash of logical thinking and were pursuing their own theme by suggesting I feed a grown man who, clearly, was not a baby.

The remainder of my thought processes were still trying to maintain their ordered behaviour by attempting to stick to the pathways of rationality. These thoughts of feeding surely were a metaphor of what was being perceived by me about the patient. Unfortunately, however, my hope that the forces of rational thinking would prevail was in vain, as the strange sensation quickly acquired a sense of certainty. Therefore I summoned my courage to tell the patient about my sensation, fully prepared to accept that my statement would only confirm the widely held belief that psychiatrists are not just doctors for the mentally ill but honorary citizens of the world of madness themselves.

I was surprised to see the patient reacting in a pensive mood, as if my comment had touched on deeper layers in his psyche. 'Yes,' was his reply; the sensation I had just described to him, was 'well-known' to him. Throughout his life he had always felt a sense of emptiness, as if he was never really 'replete'. Furthermore, his ex-wife had fulfilled the role of a 'feeding mother'. It was evident that my strange thoughts had struck a chord with the patient.

Looking at him again, I noticed once more that the size of his skull appeared too large compared to the rest of his body, even though my observation was purely based on an intuitive perception of body shapes and symmetries. I would not have taken this issue any further had my attention not suddenly been attracted by images, which appeared like slides in my mind.

What I saw in my mind were the images of starving children from the times of the civil war in Biafra where countless numbers of children with match-like skinny bodies, topped by very big heads and sad eyes, looked into a world drowned in misery.

'Is it possible that the size of your skull might be attributed to lack of food during your childhood?' I asked the patient, becoming more aware that by now a series of clues had emerged which consisted of the patient's date of birth, a 'feeding sensation', which I had had, the patient's response to it and the size of his head. Collectively these aspects pointed at an as yet unrecognised trauma, namely, the trauma of post-war starvation in childhood.

When I outlined my thoughts to the patient, he was visibly moved. He had never considered the possibility that he might have suffered from starvation in his early childhood and that the early starvation might have had a long-term impact on his whole life.

Working in the field of forensics, where the painstaking process of gathering evidence was a key issue, the patient was curious to discover how matters would develop. If my thinking was correct, the evidence available suggested that the patient had been the victim of starvation or, at least, lack of proper nutrition in his early childhood.

Certainly such a trauma would have been primarily of a biological nature. There was sufficient evidence, however, to suggest that it had left traces in his inner psychological world, too, because the patient had described a deep-rooted and lifelong sense of not being replete. I had also perceived the sensation to feed him. Having arrived at this point, I was now keen to strengthen my hypothesis through further confirmation. Three avenues for moving forward came to my mind:

1. As the patient's mother was still alive, I suggested to him to question her in as much detail as possible about his early feeding patterns.
2. As I thought there might be a possibility of obtaining an objective picture of his nutritional status in his childhood, I suggested he should have a look at his childhood photographs. The patient replied that he was not aware that such photographs existed, but was keen to search for them.
3. The patient had a sister several years younger than he. As she had been born at a time of improved living conditions in post-war West Germany, I assumed that she might not have been affected by malnourishment to the extent as my patient. If this assumption was correct then his sister should not have been affected psychologically in the way the patient had been.

The third hypothesis was confirmed immediately by the patient. Unlike him, his sister was a healthy person, living her life with a sense of feeling 'replete'. Visibly moved at the end of the first interview, the patient shook my hand and said goodbye. As far as I was concerned, I had to wait and see whether, and what, further evidence might emerge.

At the next session, the patient could hardly conceal his eagerness to report the results of his research. Questioning his mother, in as much detail as possible, had revealed that he had, in fact, been suffering from malnutrition during the first few years of his life because he had virtually been fed with food in liquid form only. As it turned out, the pieces of chocolate he had mentioned before were the exception and not the rule. His mother also remembered an interesting little detail: more than once, while sitting on his potty, he had suffered from dizzy spells, probably due to lack of food.

When he inquired about photographs, his mother replied that a photograph album had once existed. However, this was many years ago and she could not remember what had happened to it. All she could suggest was that he should search for the album in the cellar because it might have been left there years ago. The patient did so and finally recovered it.

Looking at the photographs together we saw a slim young boy with a thin body, a big head and sad eyes. Two of the patient's cousins displayed similar features.

There was not much left to be said. Sitting next to me in my consulting room in one of the most affluent countries on earth, into which the word 'hunger' only travels through the news bulletins, there was a man who, for the first time in his life, had grasped the lifelong consequences of his early exposure to hunger.

Once more the face of war had appeared. However intuitively I may have perceived the late sequelae of early hunger, the fact was that I had perceived them. I had established a hypothesis and the patient had provided the confirmation.

Establishing links between hidden symptoms of the present and an early post-war-induced trauma had produced a fruitful result. The symptom of a dizzy spell which, incidentally, was never to recur, had brought the true dimension of a post-war trauma into the open, a trauma that had been locked away in the unconscious and overlooked for more than four decades. This provided an additional stimulus to review my thinking about the question of what constitutes a symptom.

MYSTERIOUS DEPRESSION

About two years later, on a summer's afternoon, I found myself sitting in my consulting room. Opposite me sat a lady who had requested an appointment. Dealing with a variety of depressive conditions is a frequent feature of my psychotherapeutic work, but the depressed mood was not always so strikingly visible at first sight as in this lady's case. Her facial expression conveyed sadness and gloom. A slumped posture, a restless agitation and nervous twitching hands underlined the clinical picture of a depression which, not surprisingly, she found difficult to live with.

A course of antidepressant drug treatment, which she had been prescribed over the previous months, had proved useless. The patient had also undergone psychotherapeutic treatment, but had discontinued it because she had not spoken as she had 'not been able to talk about things'. Considering the situation, I did not feel very optimistic about the chances for a speedy recovery.

Looking more closely into the patient's biographical background it quickly emerged that the depression was not of recent origin. The patient told me that she had suffered from recurrent depressive episodes throughout her life. Curiously enough, these episodes had occurred particularly during the months of January and February. This year, however, for the first time, even the summer season had been overshadowed by the blight of depression. When I asked her about her own view of her illness, she stated that she had no explanation because if she knew, she 'would have improved'.

The clinical picture of her suffering was obvious. The cause of her condition, however, was unclear to me. I was tempted to believe that this patient's depression was not of an organic nature, because, for instance, there was no family history of depression, and that the depression had a psychological basis. The challenge, however, was to prove whether this hypothesis was correct. It had to be borne in mind that the patient had suffered from a lifelong history of recurrent and treatment-resistant depression without apparent clues as to the underlying cause and, so far, no response to either pharmacological or psychotherapeutic treatment.

The next step in the clinical interview would have been to elicit her family background in more detail. I would have proceeded in doing so if my mind had not been distracted by the sudden occurrence of a strange inner vision, which was very much in contrast to the atmosphere of the lovely summer afternoon.

It appeared as if my inner perception had exchanged reality for fantasy. I saw an image in which the woman sitting in front of me, and everything around, including the place and time, had been transformed beyond recognition. This middle-aged woman suddenly changed into a little girl who was crouched helplessly in a white, endless desert of snow. There was nothing else, except the little girl and the bitter loneliness of a cold winter. The girl's body, her hands, her face and even her language were frozen by the icy grip of the cold.

Faced with a patient with such a history of long-standing and unexplained depression I thought there was little to lose by conveying this chilling image to her. When I did, it struck an immediate chord with her and helped her to recall her own childhood. She told me that she had been sheltered in a children's home after fleeing from East Germany. This happened during the remorseless winter of 1944/45 when it had been freezing cold in the children's home.

Exposure to the physical cold in her early life, however, was only part of the picture. The psychological effects of coldness, too, ran like a thread through her life. Her father had been a prisoner of war in Siberia, a region not known for its hospitable climate. The feelings of coldness crossed the boundaries between body and mind, when she described her mother as a cold person. Coldness exerted such a powerful influence on her life that she felt like dying whenever the heating broke down in her flat during the winter. She mentioned that she had been struck more than once by the fact that the pattern of her depressive episodes occurred mostly during the winter months, as if to suggest a link between her condition and adverse life events.

Understanding possible links between mental problems and adverse events in individuals' lives is clearly important, as this lays out possible blueprints for change. It is equally important to then design a specific treatment strategy which will lead towards a resolution, enabling the individual concerned to shake off his or her mantle of suffering.

Inspired by the unexpected discovery of a traumatic trigger in terms of the coldness, I suggested a metaphor to the patient, which, while drawing on the image of the lonely, freezing little girl, contained the core of a therapeutic strategy. 'If,' I said to her, 'you are still sitting in the Ice Age, then it would be a matter of urgency that you thaw out as quickly as possible.'

The direct way in which I conveyed my perception of a therapeutic solution to the patient may have lacked subtlety. However, she accepted it and was curious to know more of the practical conclusions which could be deduced from my hypothesised link between the exposure to coldness in her early childhood and recurrent depressive episodes. Having little experience to draw on, I relied on my common sense and outlined a series of 'anti-cold' measures, intended to lift her mood by their 'antidepressant' effects.

I started by suggesting to her that she should wear only clothes of high quality in order to ensure that her body would not run the risk of suffering heat loss. I advised her to ensure that her blankets were of good quality for the same purpose; namely, to keep her body nicely warm throughout the whole night.

I told her to wear gloves even in the summer, if she found it helpful, and told her not to mind the looks of passers-by. Pursuing the logic of this 'anti-cold' treatment, I suggested she should have frequent and regular hot baths. Psychotherapy and physics may not have a lot in common, but I thought that this might speed up the process of 'defrosting' and free her from the grip of the so-called 'Ice Age', as I had referred to it.

If my first line of suggestions was aimed at reducing the body's exposure to the cold, I was aware that the body is only one part of the human condition. The mind and soul have to be cared for as well. Thus I advised the patient to try to create an atmosphere of warmth in her home environment. Candles could, for instance, help to achieve this with their gentle flames and soothing aura. She might also benefit from the effects of the human touch as conveyed by a gentle massage. 'This sounds good' was her brief reply, as she said goodbye to me with a spontaneous smile that brightened her face.

W. H. Auden's famous line 'Time will tell I told you so ...' crossed my mind occasionally when I wondered whether the approach I had suggested had made a difference to the patient. When I saw her again six weeks later it was clear at first sight that she looked much better. The patient reported a sudden improvement two days after the first consultation. This had lasted until now. Keeping to the 'anti-cold' strategy had maintained her sense of well-being.

She made the interesting comment that, 'Only after the first interview did I really notice how much clothing I had to wear in order to really feel warm.' This explained that despite her sensitivity to the cold she did not appear to have developed a reliable perception as to how much warmth she really required in order to achieve a sense of well-being. It also showed that she had learned a lesson about the duality of body and mind.

Now she was feeling so well that she was ready to stop her antidepressant medication. She required no further psychotherapeutic support as there was no evidence of remaining depressive features.

Undoubtedly, it would have been correct to enter the diagnosis of depression in her file. However, I felt that it was appropriate to be more precise about the nature of the patient's condition. I therefore defined this as that of a depression induced by war-related exposure to the cold. As far as the clinical progress was concerned, there had been a rapid response to the proposed 'anti-cold' therapy. As a result, a lifelong suffering had been speedily cured.

It was not the first time that I had come across links between depression and childhood trauma due to the cold of war winters. The case of the lady I have just described was, however, the most dramatic. It illustrated that the true origin of such depressions had not been diagnosed and therefore had fallen through the net of previous psychological diagnoses and care.

Both the case of war-induced hunger and of war-induced coldness in childhood conveyed a crucial message to me; namely, that it was important to be alert to new and unforeseen links between current mental phenomena and war trauma in childhood. In order to recognise such phenomena it appeared justified, if necessary, to trust hypotheses generated by unexpected inner, 'diagnostic' images more than preconceived notions about the psyche.

AN INFANT'S JOURNEY

By the late 1980s the concept of childhood war trauma as an entity had sufficiently crystallised in my mind for me to begin to explore this topic in seminars, each of which usually lasted several days. In one such seminar I was asked by a participant to assist him to be brought in touch with the emotions linked to his war experiences during infancy.

Mr G, as I shall call him, had been born in East Prussia in 1943 and was of German extraction. When barely fifteen months old, he was destined to become a refugee when his whole family, which included his parents, five older siblings and a Polish servant, were forced to flee their home village in Poland. Within a period of two months, travelling in a horse and cart, the family was to cover a distance of more than a thousand kilometres across lands ravaged by war.

Mr G knew that the journey had taken place, but this factual knowledge had remained separated from memory and emotions. Even a recent visit to Poland had not brought him closer to a perception as to how his early refugee experiences might have affected his mind at the time. He lived as if the upheaval of the flight had not entered the mainstream of his memories. Even in a long written account of his childhood that he showed me, there was hardly any reference to the drama of the flight itself, despite Mr G's degree of factual knowledge.

Sometimes slow in my responses, I did not react immediately to Mr G's initial request. Instead, I suggested he should draw out on an enlarged map the route the refugee cart had taken, using a red pencil as this would bring out the course of the route against the black and grey layout of the map. I did not give him any further instructions.

Over the next three days Mr G kept very much to himself, but on the fourth day of the seminar he told me how helpful it had been for him to draw the route. This had brought him closer to the flight experience and had touched his emotional life. This was also apparent from the sadness of his facial expression. However, his voice sounded monotonous when he talked about the Polish servant who had accompanied the family on their long journey from former East Prussia towards the West.

While Mr G talked, I listened to him in a mood that could best be described as one of detachment, not quite knowing what my attention was focusing on and what aims my thoughts were pursuing. However, after a little while I had an inkling about Mr G's accent, but was unable to pinpoint where it was from. I asked Mr G about it.

Mr G, surprised at my observation, replied that he spoke in a dialect that is common in the north-western part of Germany. His accent was, however, blended with sounds from the East Prussian dialect which the family had spoken at home. Unfortunately, integrating these two regional German sub-languages created problems for Mr G during his primary school years, as he was punished whenever the East Prussian accent became too noticeable for his teachers to tolerate.

Listening to Mr G's account, the attachment he had to the country of his origin was evident. He talked about the warmth, hospitality and simplicity of an earlier world, in which the German and Polish people had lived together in peace. How senseless the destruction of this world had been. By the time he and his family had finally arrived in the West, he had fallen so seriously ill as to be close to death.

The family had gathered around him, expecting their youngest child to die. Barely one and a half years old, he had already been given the last rites by a Catholic priest. Miraculously he survived. Having started to walk at the outset of the flight, he was unable to at the end of the journey. He had to relearn how to walk all over again.

History had pushed him on a horse and cart from a village in East Prussia to the western part of Germany. However, the flight, the crucial segment of Mr G's early life, still remained shrouded in obscurity. Mr G knew that there was a point of departure and a point of arrival, but the two months in between eluded his emotional access as if covered by the gentle blanket of 'forgetting'.

I knew only too well that there was no logical method available to me which would have enabled me to assist Mr G to reconnect to perceptions and emotions relating to the long flight. How could I hope to help Mr G to open the gate to a labyrinth of early experiences if he himself had lost the key? I knew that neither questioning Mr G nor applying hypothetical reasoning would take me any further, and I certainly knew that psychotherapists are no magicians.

Early experiences and their emotional flair may have been absorbed by us and may yet remain outside our conscious grasp. However much we may yearn for such memories to become conscious in order to experience them once more and to gain new insights of understanding, we will continue to languish in a space devoid of memories.

Sitting in my chair and not knowing any more than any of the seminar participants about what would happen, I got up and strolled across the room guided by sensations which neither seemed to be part of me nor of the logical world. I, the rational being, noticed how my hands were drawn towards objects which were either kept in my work box or which happened to be in the seminar room. However strange it may sound, I am simply describing what I experienced if I say that it felt as if it was not my mind which guided my hands, but as if my hands alone chose the various objects I collected and placed them on the carpet of the seminar room. I may have appeared more like a little child who had suddenly outwitted the seminar leader, but this did not matter to me. Inspired by a sense of confidence, I allowed my hands to proceed with what they intended to create with the various objects. I went ahead silently without talking to Mr G and simply concentrated on what I did, as it would have been pointless to comment on what I did because I would not have had the words to do so.

When I finished displaying the objects some twenty minutes later, the object arrangement covered an area of more than four square metres of the seminar room. Pieces of red string laid out in the form of a cross represented the core structure of what I had created with the objects. Four large sheets of paper, on each of which I had drawn a wheel, lay adjacent to the cross made out of string. Seen together, the red string and white sheets of paper with wheels drawn on them created the image of a cart.

At one end of the longitudinal beam of the cross, I had spread out a map of Poland showing the country where Mr G was born and which he had been forced to leave at such an early age. At the opposite end of the longitudinal beam, I placed the figure of a wooden man which was about twenty centimetres high. The figure had flexible joints and was one of those commonly used by artists for drawing purposes. I moulded its body posture to make it strike a fine balance between youthful ease and powerful strength. Throwing red string over this figure's shoulder connected it to the cart, creating a man who was pulling, if not leading, the cart with confidence and determination.

Two animal dolls sat either side of the cart – one a rabbit and the other a lion. Towards the rear segment of the cart, I placed five small pink bears. I positioned one of the tiny bears to stand at the end of the cart, looking backwards. I put sheets of A4 size paper all around the cart. All over the papers I sketched sharp, black arrows pointing threateningly at the cart as if they were flying towards it while it was moving slowly westwards, its wheels turning endlessly to cover the distance of a thousand kilometres.

While I created this scene, composed of objects, Mr G sat quietly, but following what I did with intense attention. My work with the objects and its design appeared to have captivated his imagination and he was still glancing at the silent configuration of objects when he started to talk. It was immediately obvious how much more lively, more intimate and emotionally engaged his voice now sounded compared to the way he had talked half an hour before.

There were tears in his eyes when he described that his place during the flight had been above the shaft in the front part of the cart. He said that he must have suffered from exposure to cold and been lying in his faeces. To be uprooted from his native country had been beyond his comprehension. He had been forced to flee, rather than given the choice to leave or stay.

The black arrows on the white paper, Mr G continued, symbolised the attacks, the assaults and the lawlessness of the war time. Once, he said, the cart had turned over. Horses had died, bridges had been blown up, the cold was bitter and there was a shortage of food.

The lion represented his mother. As best she could, she had shielded the children against the ferocious conditions. The father, symbolised by the rabbit, had been injured in 1939 and was too weak to take on a protective role. Despite the ordeal of their flight, the parents had kept their mutual love alive and shown tenderness towards each other.

It was the Polish servant who had walked in front of the cart. Only seventeen years old, he was more than a servant. It was he who guided the cart. It was he who searched for the routes and who became the main protector of a family who lacked a real male guardian. Such was this Polish servant's loyalty across the boundary of nationalities, that he stayed with the family even when a maid had tried to lure him back into the village where the journey started. The fact that the family survived was due to him, and he had been like a guardian angel.

The arrangement of objects had helped Mr G to recover the emotions and memories of his dramatic childhood journey. Decades had passed, but now he could feel again the emotions associated with this two-month period of his early life.

Metaphorically, the cart had not stopped rolling at the end of the war but had driven into deeper layers of Mr G's consciousness, where it influenced the way in which he perceived and conceptualised the world. To him, the cart symbolised his life. The Plough or 'Große Wagen' as it is called in German and which in its literal translation means the 'big cart', represented his favourite constellation of stars. The cover page of his own account about his childhood, which he had written a few years previously, contained virtually no reference to the flight itself, but showed a photograph of a wooden cart wheel. The image of moving was pervasive, and Mr G's report finished by stating that the purpose of existence was to be on the move – with the main aim of striving towards one's self and the selves of others.

As far as I was concerned, the work described here demonstrated the intriguing extent to which early childhood experiences were communicated and were thus perceivable, even though the individual concerned may not have been conscious of this.

It also showed the extent to which early experiences provided the breeding ground for the evolution of abstract concepts about the world. The true reality of fleeing on a horse and cart had found its metaphorical representation in the huge 'big cart' moving across infinite space alongside the Milky Way, touched by the glimmer of stars, dreams and desires.

THE DREAM OF THE WHITE STARS

A middle-aged couple wishing to overcome frictions in their relationship came to see me in order to seek professional help. Having obtained information about the background of their current stresses, I listened to the couple's discussion in order to tune in with more subtle patterns in their communicative interactions.

Listening gives me the space to absorb the flow of information and to let it glide through the landscape of my inner world. After listening for a while, I noticed an expression of anxiety on the face of the male partner, whom I shall call Mr D.

There are probably as many kinds and shades of anxiety as there are human faces to express them. What struck me this time, however, was the fact that the anxiety, as I perceived it, did not appear to correspond with the content and flavour of the ongoing discussion.

My observations may have been based on little more than a fleeting idea as they often cross the human mind when they attempt to bring some understanding into complex mental phenomena. Such an explanation would have seemed the most likely one, had I not been surprised by the sudden emergence of what looked like an inner vision.

There was not the slightest doubt that Mr D, his partner and I were sitting in my office. In sharp contrast to this reality, however, the unexpected vision introduced a new and frightening 'reality' when I 'visualised' how the white ceiling of my consulting room burst open and how a bomb or meteor fell through a gaping hole and unceremoniously crashed to the floor, not far from where I was sitting. In a way I can count myself lucky that I am no stranger to uncommon experiences. On this occasion, however, I could not avoid feeling perplexed and unable to discover any link between the reality of the session and the content of the vision as it had dawned on me. I was so perplexed that I decided to ask the couple for permission to interrupt the discussion in order to describe my vision to them.

Not surprisingly, Mr D replied, with a wry smile, that he was unable to make sense of my vision. He did, however, have the courtesy to compliment me for not being short of imagination.

Pleased for not having attracted a less favourable reply, I decided to explain to Mr D and his partner that the vision had struck me with such forceful clarity that I felt the need to search for an explanation to account for its origin.

Practising as a psychiatrist, psychotherapist and family therapist and operating in a realm between madness and normality might not be the most popular of professions, but I have always considered this to be an advantage because it offers a real opportunity and space to examine irrational strands of thinking. Over the years, I had learnt not to discount images of a seemingly senseless and illogical nature when they had formed themselves in my mind. I was therefore keen to establish whether there was any meaning to the vision described above, in terms of a possible link with past events in Mr D's life.

Once more Mr D shook his head in disbelief, but by now I observed a change in his facial expression. Without me being able to pinpoint the reason for this change, it appeared that Mr D had been affected by my account of the vision.

I urged Mr D to search his memory carefully in order to ascertain as to whether he might be able to establish a possible link between an experience in his past life and my vision. I did not have to wait for long before the torch of Mr D's memory illuminated a memorable event.

Mr D told me that at the age of two years he had witnessed an air raid. During the raid, bombs had dropped from the skies like huge, starlike objects. To be precise, numerous such air raids had taken place. On each occasion he and his family members had to seek refuge in an air raid shelter. So powerful had the impact of these experiences been on his mind at the time that he had suffered the same recurring nightmare for several years until he entered primary school. In this nightmare, huge white stars fell out of the skies directly towards him and he experienced an almighty fear that he might get killed.

Having talked about his terrifying early encounter with war from the skies, the shadow of anxiety lifted from his face. He now seemed relieved and we were able to resume the discussion at the point where I had interrupted it.

My thoughts turned to the article entitled 'Object Sculpting, Symbolic Communication and Early Experience: A Single Case Study', which I had published in the Journal of Family Therapy in 1988. In this article I referred to two object constructs, amongst others, which were part of an object arrangement of the kind described previously. Even though I did not know why I had built these two constructs, the subsequent analysis revealed a powerful link to the early childhood of the individual concerned in the sense that they symbolically reflected key elements of his two earliest childhood dreams. For months afterwards I struggled with the question as to how I had perceived key features of an individual's dreams without having possessed any previous knowledge of these dreams.

Ranking amongst the most distinctive phenomena of an individual's inner world, dreams appear to be enclosed within this inner world's sanctuary. Yet then, as in the case described above, I had 'picked up' the silent messages of the dreams. This finding suggested that, however much the interior and the exterior world seem to be separated by the concept of an impenetrable boundary, there were subtle patterns of communication that were capable of conveying information about such dreams into the outside world.

THE MEMORY OF A RIVER CROSSING

A man in his mid-fifties had come to consult me due to a negative image of himself and a growing mountain of problems. It was sad to see the spectacle of a man who felt that the future had turned its back on him and whose hope in life seemed to have evaporated like drops of rain in the desert.

My main concern was to establish a rapport with him as quickly as I could. Rather than taking him through a full clinical history straight away, I began by asking him how he was feeling now, having just entered the room of a stranger on whom he pinned expectations of being helped.

'I am still able to function,' he replied. However, having put my question to him, he was getting more in touch with himself again. This meant feeling his sadness – so much sadness – and his tiredness. While he was 'functioning' his emotions were trapped inside, like invisible lakes stretching under the surface of the desert.

Then the man – I shall call him Mr L – began to fill me in on his background. He started by telling me that he was born at the beginning of the Second World War. It was not the first time, and probably would not be the last time, that I was to hear the story of someone whose father had been taken away forever by the war. Towards the end of the war, and a short time before Mr L's father was drafted into the army, the family, including Mr L's father, had fled from an

Eastern province towards the West. At the end of the war, however, the gates of liberation did not open for Mr L' s father; instead, he found himself in a prisoner of war camp. It was here where he succumbed to a loyal companion of war — starvation.

Wars play games of dice with human lives: one person survives, another does not. Mr L' s father died, but his mother did survive. However, she suffered a mental breakdown which lasted several years. Even though her condition eventually improved, she never enjoyed a full recovery, requiring medication to keep her going for the rest of her life. Before the war, Mr L' s mother had been a beloved and happy wife. The war had taken her husband away and had made her a sad widow. This, in a nutshell, was Mr L' s family history.

While I was now trying to focus in more detail on Mr L' s personal history, a sensation preoccupied my mind which eluded my comprehension. I noticed that my thoughts started to move in circles as if looking out for the unknown.

Reviewing what had happened so far, Mr L had been born in a part of former East Prussia which is now a part of Russia. I knew that Mr L must have been five years old when he fled because he had told me his date of birth, the time of the flight and, while recounting his father's fate, he had mentioned the word 'flight'. These were clearly established facts, but it seemed as if my thoughts were taking the initiative to generate new insights without my rational mind being involved.

I told Mr L that the issue of the flight had captured my thoughts and imagination, but he looked at me in silence without responding. Only his hands made a gesture as if to indicate two levels. However, what two levels were they referring to? Why should this gesture bear any significance? And why was I paying attention to such elusive phenomena, instead of sticking to the task of obtaining more data about Mr L' s history? Why?

Suddenly the mood of uncertainty which had occupied my mind lifted, giving way to an image of lucid clarity which rose before my inner eyes. Such was the sharpness of the image that I thought I was seeing a scene cut out from reality. What lay in front of me was a white and icy area stretching endlessly. The image was of such frightening intensity that I could feel the cold creeping up my back. I could see people running across the ice. Some were closer, others resembled little more than black dots in the distance. I knew that what I saw was not a pleasant winter outing but a scene of horror, where people were running for their lives and where nobody knew whether they would make it.

I decided to tell Mr L about my vision of the white horror. 'Yes,' he replied without hesitation. He had only been five years old when he and his family had to cross an icy river on a lorry during their flight from East Prussia. It had been bitterly cold. The temperature dropped to close to −30° Celsius. Two family members were suffering from whooping cough.

While on the ice they were driving for their lives, as the fleeing refugees had been targeted by artillery fire. The shooting stopped only just before the shells reached the lorry. Thus the family was lucky to escape alive.

However, the awareness of what might have happened had they fallen into the hands of the Russians was still evident in Mr L's voice when he said that in that event his mother would have shot her own children and herself. Wars take laws like pistols into their own hands.

Half a century had passed between the war and our first meeting, but as Mr L told me there was still so much sadness. Had half a century really passed, or was it just an illusion?

A TIMELESS NIGHT

Seminars about childhood war trauma had now secured a firm place in my seminar programme. About ten participants from German-speaking countries attend each seminar and the duration of the seminars, i.e. five days, is long enough to create an atmosphere of mutual awareness, trust and support. Usually, I leave it to the individuals themselves to choose the moment when they felt ready to engage in meaningful explorations of their childhood war sagas, which often cut across the divide of consciousness and unconsciousness.

On one occasion, however, none of the seminar participants appeared to come forward. This might have worried me, but, rarely suffering from boredom, I quickly found a way of keeping myself busy by allowing my imagination to roam.

Instead of retreating into a silent monologue, I gave my fantasies the freedom to fly through the cavity of my mouth straight into the spacious seminar room.

Not considering myself a connoisseur in matters of cuisine, I found myself chatting with pleasure about the importance of food, drink and the joy of relaxing for hours at the dinner table. I spoke about a lovely house, the sense of security it provides and the homely feeling it generates. I described the beauty of a garden, the splendour of its flowers and the change of the colours brought about by the seasons. I talked about refreshing walks across the countryside where nature's miracles and wonders inspire the mind.

Yet, while chatting about such innocent matters carried me away, I felt and then saw a cloud of some inexplicable anxiety rising over the horizon of my fantasy world. This was purely a cloud which existed in my mind because there was no cloud when I looked out of the window of the seminar room. Yet it grew slowly, but relentlessly, becoming darker and more ominous. While this happened, the peaceful and idyllic themes I had chatted about were being forced out of my mind. Then I heard a noise reminiscent of approaching thunder, but again this was not real thunder but a sound generated within my mind. While it came nearer, it reminded me of the rattling noises of tanks moving threateningly towards my blissful style of life, the idyllic house and the beautiful garden.

I had already accepted the flow of fantasies, instead of fulfilling my function as a seminar leader. I became increasingly consumed by the crescendo of doom which had now narrowed to the very essentials of survival and I began to feel like a mother who knows, yes, who knows as much as anyone knows about this life …

that she has no choice left …

but to flee, …

yes, …

still during this night …

before it is too late, …

to flee with her little child …

in her arms, …

in order to try to save both their lives, …

perhaps, ...

to flee ...

towards an uncertain future, ...

if there is a future left at all ...

Then slowly the stream of fantasies was seeping away. Looking around the seminar room, I noticed that a female seminar participant had begun to cry. In fact, she was the only one crying; the others remained calm and composed. When I had succeeded in consoling her, she found words to talk about what had touched her while I had given free rein to my thoughts.

One night, at the age of three years, and without any prior warning, she had been dragged out of her bed by her mother in order to catch one of the last refugee boats to flee across the Baltic sea towards the West. In the darkest of nights of her childhood, she had been forced to leave everything behind, including her beloved doll.

Having just been in touch with the dimension of this traumatic experience, for the first time she grasped the reason for a persistent anxiety which had overcome her regularly when going to bed at night. Also, for the first time she became aware of the extent to which her lifestyle was reminiscent of a refugee existence. Having made these links of understanding, she was determined to change.

About a year later I received a postcard from Poland. For the first time since her childhood this lady had returned to her village of origin. She wrote of what an overwhelming experience it had been to recognise the colour of the sky, the contours of the village, and so many traces of her childhood. Returning to the scenes of her early life had enabled her to say a late farewell to her childhood that the ruthlessness of war had brought to such a premature end.

A MOURNING RITUAL

In history books the description of wars may create the impression of following distinct sequences of events. In seminars, however, the explorations of war traumas sometimes unfold in a manner reminiscent of a surrealistic play.

In one seminar, a participant, an athletically built man, came forward and approached me. Even though he had been born years after the end of the Second World War, he asked me if I could assist him to shed light on the psychological impact the distant war may have had on him.

My first response to his request was not very sophisticated. I just looked at him, as I did not know what to say. Eventually I had the idea of placing a wooden block in the middle of the seminar room and of putting a little toy pistol on top of it.

Then, after a while, the man whom I shall call Mr K bent down and took the pistol into his hand. Appearing lost in the silence of his thoughts, he looked at the pistol without saying a word.

Then, again after a while, he walked towards the window and threw the pistol out of the window. Coming back he stood again in front of me, tall, and although still fairly young, with the bowed posture of a man seemingly burdened by the heavy weight of an unknown legacy.

All this happened without Mr K having said a word. Of course I could now have started to ask him questions to break his silence. However, I hesitated as this did not feel right to me. Instead I started to stroll around the seminar room in circles, seemingly oblivious to what was happening, until my hands found a stack of A4-sized paper. When my hands held the white sheets of paper, I could not, at first, make sense of their intentions, but then my right hand decided to pick up a thick black pencil. Barely having grabbed the pencil, my hand started to behave as if it was guided by some kind of remote control, drawing big black crosses onto the sheets of white paper – one black cross at first, and then another one and then more and more.

Each time the drawing of a cross had been completed, my hand released the paper, letting it sail like a leaf to the floor of the seminar room until the cross had settled at a place which was determined by chance. Although I knew what my hands had done with the paper, I still failed to understand the reason for these actions.

After I had drawn some twenty crosses, Mr K was still standing in the seminar room as motionless as before. Surrounded by a growing number of nameless crosses, Mr K looked helpless, lost, and infinitely sad.

It took a while before Mr K broke his silence. Now he knew why he had become a priest he told me. He had chosen this vocation so that, in his lifetime, he could bury all those human beings whom his father had shot during the war. Even though his father had never talked openly about the war, he, Mr K, the man now standing in profound sadness in the seminar room amidst the nameless crosses, had always sensed that his father had killed other men during the war.

Mr K was born after the war and had obviously not fought like his father, who had eventually become a prisoner of war. One of Mr K's uncles had been killed in the war. However, it was left to Mr K to carry the burden of their legacy in his heart.

I told him that he could not be expected to bury the war dead on his own and that he should not demand such a task of himself. Nobody could expect him to carry out such a task without help.

One after the other, I picked up the sheets of paper and placed them in the room, laying them in a line as if I was arranging a row of graves in a cemetery. On top of each 'grave' I put a little object until they lay, each of the white sheets of paper with their dark crosses, next to each other, finally having found their resting places of eternal peace. Then, one after the other, the remaining seminar participants rose and, as if forming a silent procession, put down small signs of remembrance along the 'graves'.

There was no doubt that the war had long since finished in reality, but had it ever finished in the reality of Mr K's consciousness?

CHAPTER 2

A PARALLEL PROCESS

But it seems to me that the real answers to the cosmic mystery are to be found not in the sky, but in that other, infinitely smaller though no less mysterious firmament contained within the skull.

Johannes Kepler, in a letter to Dr J. Brengger, December 1610

SELF-OBSERVATION.
THE MAKING OF MY OWN CONSCIOUS LINKS

The clinical observations I made opened my eyes to the extent to which exposure to (post-)war trauma during and throughout childhood had shaped the minds and behavioural patterns of adults. It was to take years, however, before I was able to organise the mosaic of observations within a clear theoretical and conceptual framework.

Interestingly, the way the concepts emerged owed less to rational thinking and more to an intuitive driving force. Evolving within my consciousness, and thereby helping me to relate to, i.e. sensitising me to, my own post-war childhood, the intuitive driving force catalysed my understanding so that I could organise the mosaic of observations. By sensitising my consciousness to the existence and phenomenology of childhood (post-)war trauma in other individuals, I created an emotional, and consequently intellectual, grounding which proved of invaluable help in tuning in with and trying to conceptualise the mental phenomena I had encountered throughout my work.

The process of sensitising was fuelled by external or internal 'triggers', which provided the stimuli for the production of new insights. As the process evolved in such a self-organised manner, rational thinking hardly played a role.

A visit in the late 1980s to the German town where I had spent part of my childhood, illustrates the operation of this process. During the initial stage of my visit I was not aware of any unusual features. Within days, however, I seemed to be drifting into a frame of mind characterised by what I may describe as a perception at two different levels. While I was walking through the town centre, I noticed the shopping streets with people rushing by, lively sounds and colourful displays. Absorbing the atmosphere of modern urban life, however, represented only a segment of my experience as the propeller of my unconscious mind projected images from the past into the space of my consciousness. As if the images possessed an irresistible power, they turned my mind back to the post-war years when life in this town was still numbed from the impact of war and the shadows of a barbaric dictatorship. Black silhouettes of burnt-out façades emerged in front of my inner eyes, superimposing themselves onto modern buildings as if I were perceiving both past and present in a collage. The scores of men disabled by war, with slices of car tyres wrapped around the stumps of their amputated legs, crawled back into my memory.

The image of a man blinded in war resurfaced in my mind. Begging for money, he stood in front of a 'musical' instrument which consisted of a set of glasses, each filled with different levels of water. Letting his fingers glide slowly around the edges of the glasses, the blind man produced melancholic sounds, which now returned in their timeless fragility.

Assuming at first that such flashbacks were just a matter of coincidence, I gradually realised that there seemed to be a more methodological process at work. I recognised that this process was aimed at building a network of increasingly conscious links between my present psychological state and post-war feelings and thoughts. This networking process intensified the conscious pathways to my early experiences and widened the view over the emotional landscape of my early life. From a personal point of view this represented an enriching and illuminating development. However, of even greater importance, and of inestimable value in the years to follow, was the potential of this process for my clinical work.

This process, which had taken place in the arena of my personal space, had sharpened my perception of links between manifestations of mood states in the present and their grounding in the emotional reality of early experiences. This, in turn, enhanced my sensitivity for perceiving such links in other individuals.

Of course, it is highly relevant to recognise and identify accurately the current mood of an individual. It is even more valuable, however, if the process of identification is capable of unmasking hitherto invisible strands of connections between an individual's current mood and its roots in early life.

Fuelled by images, flashbacks and subsequent insights which occurred at random and at irregular intervals, the process of raising my conscious awareness and sensitivity occurred over several years. However, I must stress that it is an open-ended process in which new pieces continue to be added all the time to a growing mosaic of insights.

The silent self-propelling feature of the process needed time before it was connected to a language whereby the images could be embraced by words and concepts. There was a pattern of considerable delay between the purely visual and 'wordless' experience of inner images and the emergence of the ability to capture them with words. However much I saw images of the kind I have described, they seemed to remain lodged in my mind in their visual form. For a long time it appeared as if I was not able to find the right words to capture the images appropriately. Nor did I feel capable of describing my experiences from a more detached point of view.

Nevertheless, my confidence and conviction grew that the images I perceived represented a true reflection of my childhood reality rather than being the product of an imagined or virtual reality.

I am giving the following account from my personal experience in order to illustrate the points outlined so far and to highlight the role of an external trigger which, in turn, sets off states of feelings.

One summer day in the early 1980s my young son returned home soaking wet after walking in the rain. I gave him a warm shower. My son enjoyed the pleasant contrast to the cold rain and I was in cheerful mood, until my mood changed to feelings of sadness. This unexpected change caught me by surprise and, indeed, so much so that I began to wonder why this sudden mood change had occurred. I searched for an explanation over the next few weeks without being successful.

A few months later, in passing, I mentioned my curious experience to my mother, without in any way expecting that she might provide an answer. However, my little tale struck a chord with her and, reflecting on what I had told her, she remembered that as a small child, and having survived the hazards of fleeing from Eastern Europe, I had been left in the possession of just one pair of trousers. Therefore, whenever I wetted myself and my trousers were left in a deplorably wet state, my mother had little option but to put me to bed and to let me wait until the trousers had dried. When I heard my mother telling the story, there was an immediate feeling that I had never liked having to wait in bed until my trousers were dry. I sensed that this deprivation of being able to move, of space and, indeed of liberty, had adversely affected my mood at the time.

It appeared that my childhood mind had linked the experience of wetting my clothing with the unpleasant consequences of having to spend time in bed and of being deprived of freedom. The trigger of showering my son after he got soaked in the rain had reactivated a long-forgotten experience from my own childhood.

Understanding this link between an initially inexplicable depressive side of my mood and a real childhood event was, however, not the only solution to the puzzle. There was also an emotional gain attached to it because I experienced a sense of relief. Now I was in a position where I was able to weave a previously unresolved emotional thread into the tapestry of my consciousness.

This insight produced another insight, as I was now able to comprehend another, seemingly unconnected, mental experience. Even during gorgeous summer days I had often been touched by a sudden, gentle melancholy when seeing children's trousers drying on a washing line and being blown by the breeze.

The insight I obtained from this 'one trouser story' helped me to realise that the visual image of the hanging trousers had also been connected with the network of previously unconscious memories. Here, too, the melancholic aura disappeared after I became consciously aware of its childhood roots.

The process of establishing links to early experiences involved more than the mere unemotional, 'mechanical' retrieval of facts. It was crucial that the emotional flavour of the events had been reanimated, making them as close a reflection of the original experiences I had witnessed at the time through my childhood eyes.

Looking at my own emotions through my childhood eyes and not through the lens of adult rationality allowed my sensitivity to develop. The process of slowly rebuilding the links of experience to my own early post-war world provided the learning ground. Applying what I had learnt through years of mental self-observation enabled me to detect the threads of childhood (post-)war trauma within the fabric of present-day emotional states in the adults I worked with. The experience I accumulated over the years strengthened my confidence in perceiving such links. Eventually I felt encouraged to formulate a more general view, as outlined above – namely, to try to access the emotional reality of (post-)war trauma in childhood from a child's point of view, i.e. looking at the trauma through a child's eyes, rather than from an adult's perception. As so often, however, formulating an approach in theory was easier than its implemention in the complex world of clinical practice.

CHAPTER 3

COMPLEXITIES, CONNECTIONS
AND UNCONSCIOUS CONSTRUCTS

If any scientist had a nose for, to use Medawar's phrase, 'the solution of the possible,' Rutherford had. His attack was simple and direct, or rather he saw his way, through the hedges of complication, to a method which was simplest and most direct.

C. P. Snow, on the physicist Lord Rutherford, quoted in Carey (1995)

Mathematical reasoning may be regarded rather schematically as the exercise of two faculties, which we may call intuition and ingenuity ... The activity of the intuition consists in making spontaneous judgments which are not the result of conscious trains of reasoning ...

Alan Turing, quoted in Hodges (1992)

It may be that the objects around us derive their rigidity only from our certainty that they are what they are and no other, prompted by the inflexibility of thought with which we confront them.

Marcel Proust, *Du Cote´ de chez Swan*, translation by B. Green

THE SILVER NECKLACE

By the mid-1980s working with object sculpts had secured a firm place in my therapeutic repertoire of tackling the exploration of early experiences. Although I lacked an understanding of the mental processes which allowed me to carry out the construction of the often complex three-dimensional configurations of object sculpts, I found this approach extremely useful. Object sculpts enabled me to shed light on a whole range of early psychological experiences because they facilitated conscious access to them. Occasionally this also included physical trauma, findings which I have described in a series of publications (Heinl, 1987b, 1987c, 1988, 1991, 1994a, 1994b, 1998, 2000).

Increasingly, however, I observed a new dimension when working with objects. It became apparent to me that the object arrangements provided a view across the early psychological landscape of family experience, thereby facilitating an understanding of the family structures that characterised individuals' early lives. I therefore designed seminars to explore such issues in order to allow individuals to reconnect with their early family experiences.

In 1990, at the start of one such seminar, a colleague, whom I shall call Dr A, introduced himself. Referring to his medical work and his particular interest in family therapy, he expressed his desire to obtain a more thorough understanding of the atmosphere prevailing in his family during his childhood. There was nothing in any way unusual or conspicuous in the way Dr A had introduced himself. As a result, it would have been appropriate for me to thank Dr A for his introduction and to turn to the remaining participants for their introductions, in order to move forward to the next stage of seminar work.

Surprisingly, however, I found myself in a frame of mind which prevented me from allowing the introductions to continue. Without knowing what had caught my attention, my mind appeared to be preoccupied with something unknown. I was so determined to resolve this unknown issue that I was oblivious to the fact that I created the impression of a somewhat helpless seminar leader who sat quietly in his chair seemingly unable to utter a word.

Eventually I found words and turned to Dr A. I addressed him with a question about whether he wanted 'to see something'. However, as soon as I had put this question to Dr A I realised that I did not know myself what I wanted him to see. What had happened was that the question had touched my mind, seemingly arriving out of the blue, and had expressed itself in words before I had consciously realised that I lacked insight into its meaning.

As happens so often, luck and confidence played into my hands. Dr A was courteous enough not to test the meaning of my question. Also the soothing presence of an aura of confidence instilled me with the certainty that, in the end, meaning would replace mystery. Still lacking any notion of what steps I was going to take next, I got up from my chair and opened my small work case, which contains an eclectic collection of various objects. Selecting some of the objects I began to place them one by one in the seminar room. I still did not know why I had chosen these particular objects and not other ones. Proceeding in this manner, I created an arrangement of objects which covered several square metres.

All this happened over several minutes and without me having uttered a single word. Moreover, it had happened without me being able to give a rational explanation of why I had done what I had done. In an age where considerable emphasis is assigned to logical reasoning and skills, all I could say was that I felt as if my action had been guided by a clear and pervasive sense of knowing what I had to do and how to do it. Relying on this 'compass' helped me to create the object arrangement through to its completion.

Looking at Dr A, I now told him that in my view the object arrangement represented – albeit coded in a symbolic fashion – the answer to his question about obtaining a more comprehensive understanding of the atmosphere prevailing in his family during his childhood. Clear in my mind that what I had said to Dr A constituted, at worst, nothing more than a view without any rational foundation and, at best, a hypothesis which required proof, I felt it wise to add the possibility that what I had said might be regarded as 'nonsense'.

Before turning to describe Dr A's response, I would like to give a description of how the placement of the objects evolved. The first object I chose was a toy lion, about thirty centimetres in height (Figure 3.1).

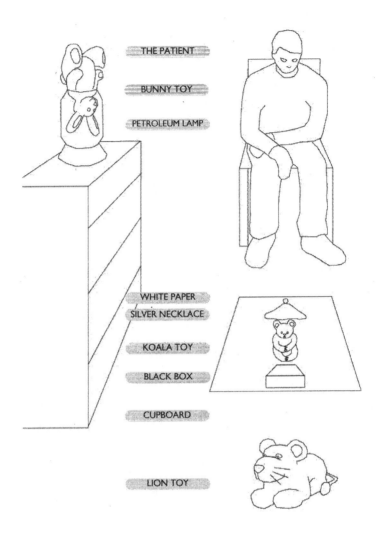

Figure 3.1 Object sculpt: the silver necklace.

I placed it at a distance of several metres from Dr A, and did it in such a manner that the lion, while standing upright, looked away from Dr A. A rabbit doll was my next choice. Even though I am usually intent on treating this animal gently, my sense of tenderness went astray when I noticed a glass cylinder of an oil lamp standing on top of a large cupboard. Without much thought, I felt compelled to force the head of the rabbit through the glass cylinder so that the poor animal stared downwards into the oil lamp, while its rear looked upwards as if floating in a glass cage between the earth and the sky.

Fortunately, however, my sense of gentleness returned when I laid out a sheet of white A4-sized paper on which I delicately placed a small pink koala bear. Just in front of this tiny animal I placed a black box embellished with fine colourful patterns. Finally, on the other side of the koala bear and still on the white paper, I laid out a silver necklace enhanced by a ruby-red stone.

Dr A had witnessed the evolution of this object arrangement without interrupting with any questions. Even after I had turned to him to convey my view that this object arrangement or object sculpt contained the answer to the question which had brought him to attend the seminar, Dr A still remained silent.

Of course, it might have been legitimate to speculate that the arrangement of childish objects in a seemingly random fashion could have left Dr A singularly unimpressed. However, even if Dr A had still not given any verbal hint as to how the construction of the object sculpt had affected him, his demeanour did. By now, it suggested a man who had been touched by what he had witnessed, who was preoccupied with his inner feelings and thoughts and who needed time to find words to articulate them. I gave Dr A the time he needed and when, after a long pause, he began to talk, he told me that the placement of the lion far away from him had affected and, indeed, scared him. Identifying the toy lion with his father, the particular way of placing the lion so far away from Dr A had reminded him of his father's long work-related absences.

A first link had now been established between a component of the object sculpt and a member of Dr A's family of origin, namely, his father. Dr A continued in this vein by saying that the small pink koala bear reminded him of himself. In particular, the fact that the koala bear was left standing on its own evoked memories in Dr A of often having been 'locked away' in what is called a *Ställchen* in German, namely, a wooden play pen to keep children from harm.

It was clear that Dr A recounted these memories of loneliness with sadness. While reconnecting with those early experiences, he felt a sensation of wanting to hide in the black box and to close its lid, only allowing a strip of light to get through it.

Having now made links between two toy animals in the object sculpt and two family members – Dr A's father and himself – it did not appear surprising that Dr A identified the rabbit as representing his mother. However tempting such a step of identifying might have appeared at first sight, it seemed somewhat more challenging to match the unusual placement of the rabbit with the real-life figure of Dr A's mother. Indeed, if the way the rabbit had been placed carried any, albeit symbolic, meaning it would have to find its reflection in the persona of Dr A's mother.

Not surprisingly Dr A stated that it was difficult for him to see a parallel between the rabbit and his mother. Unlike his father, his mother had always been at home and he therefore found it difficult to see why the rabbit should have been placed at a distance from the koala bear. He was also puzzled by the meaning of the strange and enforced locked-up position of the rabbit.

At first sight Dr A's objections did seem convincing. However, when I pointed out to him that the emotional experience of closeness or distance is not necessarily linked to physical closeness or distance, Dr A conceded that there had always been a sense of emotional distance between himself and his mother – notwithstanding the fact that she had always been at home.

Exploring in more detail how Dr A's mother had strived to fulfil her maternal role it emerged that she had been guided by the principle of duty towards her children. Rather than being filled by warmth and joy in seeing her children grow and develop, life had been a 'burden' to her. Hidden behind the mask of duty, the dimension of constraint and inhibiting forces had become perceptible – making the symbolic link to the rabbit's fate easy to recognise.

Interestingly, another facet of the dimension of constraint emerged when Dr A stated that the rabbit in the glass cylinder also reminded him of his maternal grandmother. She had lived above the rest of the family in their family house. She had also exerted her rule over them due to her dominant personality.

However playful and devoid of any rational content the object sculpt and its evolution may have appeared to any observer, the subsequent dialogue between Dr A and myself had brought to light a surprising and striking network of links between the symbolic meaning of the object sculpt and Dr A's family of origin. Furthermore, the object sculpt had provided insights into the structure of Dr A's family of origin and had generated a sense of the atmosphere prevailing in his family. Although the construction of the object sculpt had evolved without any rational deliberations or planning on my part, it had achieved its objective, namely, of providing Dr A with a greater understanding of the atmosphere in his family. All this had happened within the context of a first encounter, in the absence of any information about Dr A's family of origin and within the course of about half an hour.

Despite the fact that no logical processes seemed to be involved, it would have been difficult to entertain the notion that the processes which had occurred were little more than the product of random influences. In fact, at least for me, it was obvious that a highly sophisticated system had been in operation, whose aim consisted of converting perceptions into insights through the use of objects. However little I seemed to comprehend of how these processes proceeded, I had to admire the way in which subtle patterns of communication conveyed by another human being were translated into the object-sculpt-texture of new insights.

I gave in to a brief interlude of reflection on the revelations which had just taken place and I felt the time had now come to signal to the remaining seminar participants that they should continue with their introductions.

I was about to do so, but when I looked once more across the landscape of the object sculpt, whose silent language had conveyed so much, I noticed that there had been one object which had been left without having been specifically referred to – the silver necklace. First, wondering whether this was really of any significance, I decided to draw attention to the necklace by mentioning that it was of Bohemian origin. Fully aware that this represented only a casual comment, I did not lose much time to venture into the area of speculation by asking Dr A whether his parents originated from the Czech Republic. I can only emphasise how much I was aware that what I had said constituted little more than a hypothesis, virtually drawn from nowhere. If there was someone who should have been embarrassed by Dr A's answer — namely, that his parents did not come from the Czech Republic — then this was clearly me, as I should not have articulated a hypothesis based on such shaky grounds.

Having been taught a lesson, I should have exerted more control when the next question entered my mind. I am sure I would have succeeded in doing so had this second question not lodged itself in my mind with such clarity and certainty as if to require no further proof. I addressed Dr A once more, this time asking him whether his parents had been refugees. Once again, I was prepared to see this question dismissed.

However, whereas Dr A had denied my previous question with a smile, his facial expression now showed a change to sad thoughtfulness when he replied that both his parents had been refugees from former German settlements in Eastern Europe. In fact, one parent had originated from an area close to the Bohemian border.

When I put it to Dr A that having had two refugee parents had made him, in a way, a refugee child, he looked at me somewhat surprised, saying that he had never seen the implications of his parents' refugee fate in this way.

Once more the necklace grabbed my attention, inspiring me to ask Dr A whether his mother had taken a necklace with her when she was fleeing. Dr A confirmed this hypothesis, saying that a necklace had been the only piece of jewellery she had taken with her. However, later on in her life his mother had never worn this necklace again.

The small detail of the necklace had added a significant dimension to the understanding of the dynamics and atmosphere of Dr A's family of origin. It highlighted the burden and traumatic repercussions of the refugee experiences on the emotional matrix of the family. Dr A concluded by saying that he had already been aware of some aspects of what had been brought to light during the work with the objects. However, never before had he experienced such a panoramic view of the core issues of his family background.

Having described the work with Dr A from my point of view, I was interested to learn in more detail about how Dr A had perceived the object sculpt from his own perspective. Dr A kindly provided an account in which he noted the experiences and feelings he felt as a result of the object sculpt. The quotations which follow, and translated by me, came from Dr A's account, which complements the observations and insights I have described.

Dr A started his account by referring to the first object I used, namely, the lion. He described experiencing 'a spontaneous impulse to turn the lion's head round instead of letting it stand in the corner as if punished'. Seeing the rabbit being squeezed head down into the oil lamp cylinder on top of the cupboard did strike him 'as being comic, but also odd and even somewhat crazy'. This situation, too, evoked an impulse in Dr A to remove the rabbit from its cage and to bring it down. This impulse intensified when the pink koala bear was placed on its own in the middle of the seminar room on a white sheet of paper. Looking at the little bear, which appeared alone, made 'me sad and brought back associations reminding me of the "Ställchen". Fantasies and memories of my parents emerged. I remembered how they were in some way absent and very busy. My father had his job and also participated in voluntary work. My mother ran the household and looked after the children ...

'When you asked me the question whether my mother had loved life, I realised that she had never really liked her work. This was a view new to me and made me sad because it reinforced a familiar perception, namely, the extent to which we children were a great burden to my parents. Then you added a black box. I would have liked to hide the pink koala bear in the box – not in order to bury it inside the box, as you speculated, but in order to protect it. Then you laid the silver necklace with the ruby stone on the paper. At first I had no idea what to make of the necklace until the Bohemian origin of the necklace provided the trail, leading to the refugee background of my parents. Both arrived in former West Germany without any possessions. My mother arrived soon after the end of the Second World War whereas, in contrast, my father came only after years of having been a POW in the former Soviet Union ... The necklace which my mother never wore was one of the few belongings from my parents' country of origin. You asserted that my parents might have been psychologically absent in their post-refugee environment because they had remained too attached to their country of origin and because they had been unable to overcome its loss. This touched me profoundly. At this moment I experienced the full dimension of family issues relating to the refugee drama.

'I felt how much in terms of isolation, how much of having to adjust and adapt oneself, had determined the family atmosphere. I realised how much anticipated rejection there had been, which would then, in fact, materialise − like a self-fulfilling prophecy. Suddenly I became emotionally and existentially aware of having had a place where I lived, without having had a native country. It was a relief for me to hear you saying that not every problem had to be understood from an intrapsychic perspective.

'There were issues which were the consequence of real events. Some facets of my problems seem to me due to the impact of the refugee tragedy on my family. The parents who had been uprooted and traumatised had been shattered in their self-esteem. I could now clearly see the repercussions these events had on me.

'You suggested to me, I should invite my parents to come on a journey to visit their country of origin. I found this encouraging and felt that it aimed towards integrating the family history and helping to achieve a greater sense of "grounding" and connection when entering into this emotionally cut-off, repressed, unloved and painful part of my family history, because the feeling of displacement and alienation had been so much a feature of the family's history.

'Working with you brought an important theme to the surface, a theme which I had found myself standing on insecurely throughout my life. What surprised me was the fact that the work with the objects and the dialogue had gradually unravelled the emotional and also existential importance of the issue, ... the idea of describing myself as a refugee child had never entered my mind. During and after working with you a series of intense feelings and memories crystallised. My parents' history has become clearer to me and due to this I have had the ability to engage in more discussions with them.

'I can see how all this refers to me … as I have become more aware of the important role of integrating the family history. I feel a sense of belonging to two home countries, even if they are separate entities, namely, the old and the new one.'

As a result Dr A had recognised the traumatic patterns which had had a deep impact on his family. They included the sense of isolation, the need to have to prove themselves constantly, the anticipated rejection felt by others and the emotional absence from his parents. He recognised, too, that these patterns had been due to a force which had long escaped his attention: the scourge of war.

THE ENIGMA OF THE DESERT

There is a widespread belief that the access to early life experiences in adults requires the framework of a long-term therapeutic relationship and the use of language in order to allow unconscious material about early life experiences to 'break' into consciousness. My observations, however, pointed increasingly in a different direction. Relying on intuitive perception and thinking and a growing sense of confidence enabled me to turn the telescope of observation towards the space of early experiences. Sometimes, when looking at what had materialised in the course of such work, I could not help feeling a sense of amazement and wonder when issues that had been hidden for decades in the landscapes of unconsciousness emerged suddenly before my eyes.

This is illustrated in the following seminar work with a woman, whom I shall call Mrs R, a psychologist, who was in her late thirties. This work, too, took place in the mid-1980s during a five-day seminar that was designed to explore early life experiences. The twelve participants were mainly mental health professionals. Mrs R's motivation in attending the seminar was not due to a wish to explore her childhood or a war issue.

Mrs R had lived in a stable relationship for the last six years and had no children. Her thoughts were very much focused on exploring her ambivalence towards her desire to have children. This ambivalence had overshadowed a previous pregnancy. While living in the relationship she referred to, she had recently become pregnant for the first time in her life despite the use of contraception. Later on, Mrs R took the difficult decision to undergo an abortion, which was carried out six months prior to the seminar. In addition, Mrs R mentioned that a previous sixteen-year relationship had resulted in her being childless as she had taken 'perfect precautions'.

While Mrs R gave her account, and I like to emphasise that there had been no previous consultation, I raised a few more questions concerning her relationships during adulthood. However, it did not take long before it became apparent to me that Mrs R's request – although easily defined – posed a complex problem because it touched on the issue of ambivalence. Obtaining the impression that further exploration through verbal dialogue was unlikely to prove successful, my attention turned towards examining the problem through intuitive perception, thinking and the use of objects, with the hope that these instruments might lead to a more promising outcome.

As Mrs R continued with her account, I surrendered to the dynamics of intuitive forces like a sail surrendering to the wind. I placed a variety of objects, one after another, in the seminar room. It was not the first time that the eventual arrangement of the object sculpt, which covered a large area of the seminar room, must have made a somewhat bizarre impression on any observer (Figure 3.2).

To start with I placed a series of wooden blocks along a straight line (see bottom of Figure 3.2). Then I added two toy animals, a rabbit and a lion. Standing at a distance from each other the two toy animals did not look at each other. Please note that in the illustration the animals have been turned so as to be recognisable to the reader. They both looked towards other objects which were going to be placed in front of them, such as a glass filled with red herbal tea and, a little bit further down to the right, a green spruce branch and to the left a branch of red rowan berries. Beyond these objects, I created an area composed of seemingly 'dead' objects in matt colours. In the middle of the objects, I placed a sharp stone which was surrounded at the edges by a collection of dry branches and pale brown cones. Further down the room (see top of Figure 3.2) two brightly

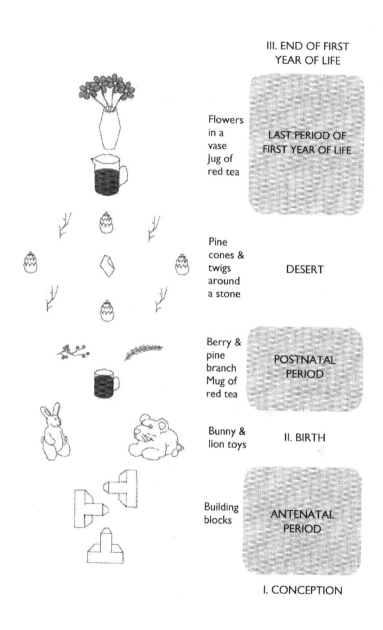

III. END OF FIRST
YEAR OF LIFE

Flowers
in a
vase
Jug of
red tea

LAST PERIOD OF
FIRST YEAR OF LIFE

Pine
cones &
twigs
around
a stone

DESERT

Berry &
pine
branch
Mug of
red tea

POSTNATAL
PERIOD

Bunny &
lion toys

II. BIRTH

Building
blocks

ANTENATAL
PERIOD

I. CONCEPTION

Figure 3.2 Object sculpt: the enigma of the desert.

coloured objects enlivened the display. These were a glass teapot, again filled with intensely red herbal tea and then, at the end, a pot filled with vivid flowers.

Having completed the object sculpt I was, of course, aware that I had constructed it without the application of logical thinking. I was even more aware that its meaning, if it possessed any at all, and its relevance to Mrs R's problem, was highly questionable. Indeed, given the curious way in which the object sculpt had developed, what kind of meaning could such a strange and seemingly random assembly of objects possess?

However, with a stubborn sense of confidence, I indicated to Mrs R that the object sculpt, which I had just completed in front of her eyes, bore a relation to her problem in the sense that it conveyed an answer to it – albeit in a symbolically coded fashion.

While I was still occupied with the question of the symbolic meaning of the object sculpt, I developed a sudden hypothesis that it might be a metaphorical representation of Mrs R's first year of life. Surely one might have expected Mrs R to be at a loss with what lay in front of her eyes, unable to comprehend what the object sculpt signified. Yet, judging by the intensity with which she looked at the seemingly random collection of objects, she appeared captivated by what I had constructed in front of her. In fact, it did not take long before Mrs R, too, realised that the 'silent language' of the objects conveyed her first year of being alive.

Later she wrote an account, in which she captured the very first moment of attaching a meaning through words to the object sculpt: 'The beginning of the object sculpt was clear. The lion and the rabbit, who represented my father and my mother, were separate. Towards the centre of the object sculpt there was the scarcity, the desert. *Without knowing at that moment, I felt this was my first year of life. The desert was most important.*'

Having received a surprisingly speedy confirmation for my hypothesis, it seemed logical to explore whether any further meaningful links could be found between individual parts of the object sculpt and Mrs R's early life experiences. With this aim in mind, a dialogue developed between Mrs R and myself.

However, having established a meaning for the whole of the object sculpt implied a leap of imagination by introducing the dimension of time into it. If the spatial arrangement of the objects across the seminar room represented Mrs R's first year of life, then they had to be viewed against an invisible time axis along which the objects were positioned. Encouraged by previous work, which I described in my paper 'Object Sculpting, Symbolic Communication and Early Experience: A Single Case Study' (1988), I felt confident that the strategy of introducing the time dimension might prove fruitful in Mrs R's case, too. Therefore I assumed the time axis to run from the bottom of Figure 3.2 to the top. Further, I assumed that the series of wooden blocks at the bottom of the figure might represent Mrs R's beginning of her life – namely, the antenatal period – and that Mrs R's birth was indicated by the point at which the rabbit and the lion dolls stood.

If this was the starting point of Mrs R's life, then it followed that the remainder of the object sculpt reflected the development of Mrs R's first year of life up to its end (III in Figure 3.2). I was aware of the speculative nature of my assumptions and that the introduction of the time axis would test these assumptions. If, for instance, individual objects did convey specific meaning that was relevant to this early period of Mrs R's life, then this meaning had to relate to a point in time during the first year of her life where the individual object was placed. There was little else I could do, except to wait and see how matters would unfold.

From her first impression Mrs R had identified the object sculpt as representing her first year of life, and the lion and rabbit doll as symbolic representations of her parents. In doing so, Mrs R had, in effect, construed a meaning that related to her early life history. The object sculpt appeared to have acted as a trigger in connecting the perception of visual objects to early experiences. I was therefore curious to see how the subsequent analysis of the object sculpt would evolve.

Figure 3.2 shows the lion and the rabbit doll placed at a distance from each other. Their faces were directed towards the objects laid out in front of them, and there was no eye contact between the lion and the rabbit doll. This may have been a coincidence or simply immaterial. However, Mrs R spontaneously commented that this arrangement between the toy animals reflected the nature of the relationship between her parents, which was cold and distant. Due to the object sculpt, further evidence to that effect emerged when Mrs R remembered that her younger sibling had to sleep for years between the parents in their bed. However, despite the distance between her parents, Mrs R felt strongly that they both wanted to have her. There was factual evidence to support this perception, as her mother had consulted her family doctor more than once in order to seek his advice on how to become pregnant.

At the start of the object sculpt I had laid out several wooden blocks that created a lifeless and barren impression. If, indeed, this segment of the object sculpt represented Mrs R's antenatal period then the deprived impression of it seemed to contradict the notion of a fulfilled pregnancy because Mrs R was certain that she had been a wanted child. However, Mrs R now remembered that her mother's pregnancy with her had been overshadowed by sadness, if not depression. She remembered photographs showing her mother's sadness during that time.

After this encouraging start, the search for meaningful links between the object sculpt and Mrs R's early life moved on towards the postnatal period. Here, objects radiated a colourful contrast to the pale wooden blocks that had been placed before them; for example, a glass filled with red herbal tea, a green spruce branch and a branch with red rowan berries. These objects provided a colourful and charming arrangement, but did they contain any meaning which might be relevant to Mrs R's first year of life?

Relying on my imagination, I hypothesised that the sparkle of these objects might indicate that Mrs R's postnatal period had been a cheerful and happy one. This view was immediately confirmed by Mrs R. Clearly a meaningful link appeared to have been established between this set of three objects and Mrs R's happy account of her postnatal period. I was now interested to see whether more specific meaningful links could be discovered between each of these three objects and aspects of Mrs R's early life.

I did not have to wait long for answers to emerge. Mrs R stated, having been born in the spring, that the small green spruce branch reminded her of the time when her mother had frequently taken her to nearby forests and open fields in a pushchair during the first few months of her life.

The other two objects – the glass filled with tea and the berries – made me wonder whether they might refer to nutritional experiences in Mrs R's early life. I suggested to Mrs R that the tea in the glass represented liquid nourishment, that is, milk from the breast, while the berries stood for solid food. However, what I had not quite accounted for was the fact that such an idea would create an intricate problem, as it challenged the concept of the time axis. Bearing in mind its existence, the change from milk coming from breastfeeding to solid food, e.g. berries, would have occurred at the rather early stage of only 2–3 months.

Not surprisingly, Mrs R seemed less than convinced by this hypothesis. This wariness towards my hypothesis certainly pointed to the fact that she preserved her own judgement throughout the process of analysing the object sculpt. In order to clarify this issue, I therefore suggested to Mrs R that she should try to obtain further independent information from her mother about the pattern of her early nutrition. Mrs R was willing to contact her mother, who confirmed, to Mrs R's surprise, that she had, indeed, breastfed Mrs R, but only until the age of about 2–3 months. Under rare circumstances, Mrs R was put on solid food, which included potatoes and cabbage, in contrast to her younger sibling who was breastfed for much longer. Having had no conscious recollection of these facts regarding her early life, Mrs R was clearly stunned by these discoveries. I, too, was left intrigued by these revelations which had been brought to light by the selection of objects and in the absence of logical thinking.

Moving further along the object sculpt, and paying attention to the time axis, there was now a fairly wide area whose colourless features were in visible contrast to the sense of vibrancy conveyed by the three objects just left behind. A stone lay in the middle of this area. It was surrounded by some dead branches and dry pine cones, which were scattered around. Although this section of the object sculpt seemed to exude a desert-like quality, it had nevertheless captivated Mrs R's imagination right from the start.

Furthermore, this desert had weighed so intensely on Mrs R's mind that she described a sense of relief, later on, when she noticed that the flowers were placed at the other end of the desert. If what had been established so far was anything to go by, then the area of the desert was likely to correspond to a phase in Mrs R's early life which must have started when she was 2–3 months old. Viewed against the time axis, this phase must have lasted for several months. If any psychological meaning could be deduced from the desert-like atmosphere of this particular area, then it might, to my mind, have suggested an extended period of her early life, which was bare and cold and lacking *joie de vivre*. If the observations described in my above-quoted publication were anything to go by, then the desert-like atmosphere might even point to a period of early 'depression'.

Such a view was easily expressed, but how could it be proved? My aim was to find the answer to what may have caused the warm and lively environment to change so drastically into an emotionally deprived landscape. I asked myself the question: If the 'desert' was a metaphorical display of this phase of Mrs R's early life, then what was the nature of this experience?

There was no lack of questions, but there were no answers because Mrs R did not appear able to provide an explanation that would have seemed appropriate for the metaphorical representation of a 'desert'. However, there was at least one important piece of evidence available which suggested that the 'desert' was not a fiction of my imagination: Mrs R was positive that the 'desert' reflected her perception of what really happened during her infancy. Having formulated the above hypothesis, the task now was to try to solve the following problem. How could events – possibly traumatic events – have had an impact on Mrs R's infant mind in such a way as to leave the mental imprint of a 'desert' in her adult mind?

I inquired systematically about a whole spectrum of possible scenarios which might have accounted for such a result. I asked Mrs R whether she had experienced an early loss, separation, illness, hospitalisation or whether she had been placed in a children's home, but these possibilities were quickly ruled out by Mrs R as causes for the desert-like emptiness she felt in her adulthood. It had not occurred to me to enquire about the possible impact of war. In the end, it appeared that there were no adverse life events which would have affected Mrs R's infancy or her mother's life at the time. Furthermore, given the fact that Mrs R had been a wanted child, there seemed little support for the notion that the attitude of Mrs R's mother towards her infant daughter should have changed after the first couple of months.

The possibilities seemed increasingly exhausted, but then the idea occurred to me that Mrs R's mother might have suffered an as yet unexplained stress when Mrs R was an infant. Mrs R had been a wanted child, but maybe there was the paradoxical chance that the experience of Mrs R's mother interacting with her first child might have 'stirred up' an unresolved trauma in Mrs R's mother, thus leading to a deterioration of her capacity for maternal care. Having ventured a long way out on the thin ice of speculation, I speculated further that such a decline might not have manifested itself clinically; that it could have been more subtle, yet of sufficient strength to cloud the developing internal world of the infant in such a way as to leave shadows behind, well into adulthood.

Of course, I was aware of the possibility of having created a speculative 'house of cards'. Yet all was not yet lost. I asked myself, what if Mrs R's mother had suffered an early trauma or traumas in her own childhood, which had never been resolved and whose unhealed wounds were opened up by the experience of caring for her own infant daughter? Would it be beyond imagination to make such a transgenerational leap over more than six decades? How would it be possible to prove that such trauma(s) had happened in the early life of Mrs R's mother? I did not know the answer, but I was aware that the testing ground for proving such a hypothesis had suddenly shifted decades into the distant past by linking early events in Mrs R's life to the early world of her mother.

It very quickly emerged that one of the first associations Mrs R had made when she looked at the object sculpt was when it triggered her memory of the early death of her maternal grandmother, who had died of encephalitis when Mrs R's mother was only nine months old. Thus the highly speculative possibility was confirmed that Mrs R's mother had suffered a traumatic loss in infancy which led to her being raised by her relatives.

This was, however, far from the complete story. In essence, it was only the beginning in unravelling a maze of unresolved issues. When I inquired about Mrs R's maternal grandfather, she stated that she did not know anything about him, except the fact that he had been killed during the First World War. Although Mrs

R did not know when or where he had died, it was now established that Mrs R's mother grew up as an orphan, as she had lost both parents early on in life. It was only after the seminar that Mrs R was able to find out the exact circumstances surrounding her grandfather's death.

Mrs R's grandfather had been drafted into the German army at the outbreak of the First World War, when his wife (Mrs R's grandmother) was pregnant with his child (Mrs R's mother). Sadly he was never to see his wife again and never to see his daughter. Mrs R described in moving terms how she sat down with her mother to read the affectionate and loving letters which her grandfather had sent to his wife from the battlefields.

However, as time went on, the tone of the letters became increasingly distressed until the letters ended altogether when Mrs R's grandfather was killed in action. This was witnessed by a fellow soldier. It was then that Mrs R discovered for the first time where her grandfather died. He died in Syria, in the desert ... The enigma surrounding the 'desert' was finally solved.

The evidence of the early loss of both parents, which affected Mrs R's mother, supported the notion of a transmission of early traumatic experiences across a generation, a so-called transgenerational effect. Witnessing the new life with her infant daughter had seemingly reactivated an unresolved unconscious trauma in Mrs R's mother, which, in turn, had overshadowed Mrs R's early life.

The metaphor of the desert which was relevant to Mrs R's early life also reflected the emptiness caused by the traumatic losses in her mother's early life. It also represented the image of the real desert which had cut her grandfather's life short. Decades shrank as the distant tragedies became painfully palpable and present in the seminar room.

There were only two remaining objects which needed to be decoded. They lay at the end of the object sculpt. The impact of the 'desert' area affected Mrs R so deeply that she expressed a sense of relief when, in contrast, she noticed in front of her at the end of the time axis these two colourful objects placed towards the end of her first year of life (see Figure 3.2, top). The atmosphere created now was one of renewed vigour, which was conveyed by the dark red colour of the rose hip tea and the intensely coloured blossoming flowers. This reflected Mrs

R's perception of a warm emotional climate, which was noticeable towards the end of her first year of life.

The resulting reason for Mrs R's emotions being uplifted could not be evaluated by Mrs R. She did not know why she felt a sense of relief after having mentally 'crossed the [metaphorical] desert'. Mrs R said she believed that her aunt played an important role in supporting her emotionally.

Following my suggestion, Mrs R produced a drawing of her first year of life based on her own perception. The composition of this visual representation offered a striking similarity in terms of content and timing to that which I had arranged through the object sculpt, without me having had any prior knowledge of Mrs R's first year of life.

Mrs R represented her mother by drawing a brown circle on a piece of paper. Next she drew a brown line which represented Mrs R's mother's pregnancy. The colour brown was used to depict her mother's frame of mind. It represented the sadness she felt during her pregnancy. Following this, a red circle was drawn with blue colours inside it. This displayed a symbol which she defined as being her and her perception of having been a very much wanted child. The subsequent segment of the drawing encapsulated the feeling of a postnatal period, which was lively and radiant. This was represented by the symbol of a horizontally rising red life line and by other symbols such as musical notes.

The exuberant spirit, however, faded, when the 'life line' fell and the symbols disappeared, giving way to the lonely landscape of the desert. However, there was a re-emergence of vitality which occurred towards the end of the first year of her life. Two big hearts and two plants symbolised a new ascent of life reminiscent of the immediate postnatal period.

Mrs R later provided a written account of her experience after having seen the object sculpt for the first time. She stated, that 'Without knowing … I had the feeling that the object sculpt was the representation of the first year of my life. The desert was most important. Soon afterwards, I remembered that my mother had lost her own mother through death at an age when my mother was very young. I also recalled that after my abortion I had briefly talked in my therapy session about my thoughts that a child would have confronted me with my own early experiences. Observing the display of the objects and the desert ... had simply a calming effect on me.'

Mrs R's account illustrated that crucial elements of the transgenerational network of trauma already occupying her mind had been evoked by the object sculpt experience. Instead of the object sculpt having a weak and short-lived effect on Mrs R, it had a strong one. The object sculpt affected her consciousness and triggered emotions. It unveiled a new dimension whereby Mrs R faced a prolonged process of realising the truth of events in her childhood, which previously had been idealised in her mind. This process, in particular, catalysed her working through the sadness relating to her infancy, which had up until now been unresolved.

In her own account she stated: 'Contrary to all logic, I had idealised the earlier phases of my life. I used to attribute my mental stability and good physical health to the fact that I had been a wanted child. This belief began to be shaken when my mother conceded that she had become aware of how little she had caressed us because she herself had received so little. After the seminar ended, a period of great sadness commenced ... I saw myself as completely deficient. At first I tried hard to bring this process of mourning to an end. I had thought, up until this point, that I knew everything. This approach, however, failed and for a long time I felt left without strength and exhausted.'

However, over the course of several months, Mrs R's sadness gradually gave way to a feeling of strength. Changes took place. She questioned her tendency to fulfil other people's needs rather than her own ones. She established clearer boundaries *vis-à-vis* her family of origin. She became more conscious of what she could and what she could not expect and managed to take the idealised relationship she had formed over the years towards her father and sibling and viewed it more realistically. As far as the relationship to her mother was concerned, there were more conversations about her mother's early life, including her reading her grandfather's letters with her mother.

To conclude, in Mrs R's experience the object sculpt had achieved several objectives. The objects had allowed Mrs R to see a symbolic interpretation of her early life. This was encapsulated in the time-space structure of the object sculpt. The object sculpt had determined definite links between the meaning of the individual objects and specific early experiences. The experience of the object sculpt revealed an important pattern of transgenerational transmission of early traumas, placing the metaphor of the desert in a transgenerational context. Making links between unresolved childhood issues and the present had helped Mrs R to understand the roots of her ambivalence towards pregnancy better because some time later Mrs R wrote to me saying that she was pregnant, and that she was enjoying her pregnancy.

The enigma of the desert had been solved. The desert no longer blurred and confused her mental state. She no longer felt the emptiness and bareness that she had previously felt. However, war had again played a distant role in an individual's life. The links with war had been so difficult to detect that they had nearly succeeded in preventing new life from flourishing.

A JOURNEY INTO THE ABYSS OF CONSCIOUSNESS. THE STORY OF A CHILD WITNESS

'Whenever I recall the time when we fled, I always experience a cold sensation,' stated a woman of nearly sixty years who wrote to me in the summer of 1999, 'I always feel cold. My feet turn as cold as ice. Nothing helps me to keep warm. My nice woollen socks make no difference to this feeling I get. When I look outside, the summer landscape which is filled with illuminating green trees and vibrant flowers … suddenly turns white.'

Her letter continued: 'Our flight began on 26th January 1945. To be exact, it may have started a bit earlier or later as the Nazi connections of my parents had secured us tickets for a journey with the Wilhelm Gustloff cruiser. However, a divine intervention, which took the form of a gall bladder colic, forced my mother to bed, making it impossible for her to travel [thus saving their lives, as the Wilhelm Gustloff was subsequently sunk with thousands of refugees on board]. I was staying at my grandmother's in a neighbouring village and suddenly I was called home in order to care for my mother.

'Suddenly we got a telephone call,' the woman continued in her letter. 'I was told to go down the road to my aunt's house. I was told to tell my aunt to pack her belongings, in order that she could leave Danzig that same evening, on the last available train. My grandmother was also told by phone to leave.

'The women planned to go to the railway station, taking their children with them. As soon as my grandmother arrived, we all set out with our sledge, which was loaded with baggage. On the way to the railway station we collected our aunt and my cousins. While the other three children sat on the sledge, on top of the baggage, I was obliged to walk alongside my mother, aunt and grandmother.

'There was a lot of snow; half a metre high. I often stumbled and fell into the snow. This made my mother shout at me that I was "a big girl", although I was only five years old. Throughout the flight I was to remain as my mother's "big girl" and also as "her support", the one on whom she could "count on". When I compared myself to my younger cousin, it was quickly pointed out to me by my mother that she was fourteen months younger than I was.

'When we boarded the train, there was complete darkness. For safety reasons we occupied a compartment next to the door, although it happened to be particularly draughty there ... As far as I can remember, we went to sleep in the luggage racks. Suddenly we were woken up by loud voices urging us to get back into the railway station. There were some straw mattresses lying on the floor of the railway station. It was not possible to leave Danzig [Gdansk], as Polish partisans were surrounding the railway station. We stayed inside the station waiting room. Little children were playing "Brüderchen, komm, tanz mit mir" [Little brother come and dance with me] from the Opera "Hansel and Gretel" by Humperdinck to pass their time. This had been playing at the Danzig Opera house. To this day I remember the final stage set with its illuminated Christmas tree.

'The second night we again stayed in the train, but then we had to get off the train and sleep on the floor of the station. The following day, my grandfather brought a sack filled with loafs of bread and sausages. In this manner we had to struggle along for about a week and only now do I understand why I still find it impossible to prepare sandwiches for little journeys. I cannot recall exactly when the train finally managed to depart from the encircled town.

'I do, however, clearly remember that it was very dark. Everybody had to be as quiet as mice. To prevent the children from screaming or sobbing, scarfs were tied around their mouths; really tightly. For once, I was treated as a child, and had to put up with a scarf pressing hard against my mouth. The woollen fibres nearly suffocated me. Attempting to swallow them made me feel sick. Eventually, I managed to get rid of this tormenting garment.

'The train only travelled short distances. It moved very slowly, sometimes at a snail's pace. There were even instances when it moved backwards. In any case it was only on the 2nd of February that we finally arrived on the island named Usedom, an island in the Baltic Sea north of Stettin [Szczecin]. The journey had lasted for five days and was beset by problems. Babies' nappies were smelling foul. "Washing" had been reduced to the absolute minimum. Most of it was done in the mornings in the cold snow. We were restricted to only washing our hands and faces. Because of the cold temperatures we never could take off our clothes. To prevent outside detection from sparks or lights, the train was neither heated nor illuminated. The days may not have lasted long during this winter time but the nights were most miserable. In order to relieve oneself one had to wait until the train had stopped. Whether the train would really stop or for how long was, however, never certain. Due to these circumstances, anxieties arose as people were scared to venture out from the train in case it left at any time without them.

'When I remember these events I always feel alone. My grandmother held my brother in her arms; he was wrapped up in my mother's fur coat. My mother was busy with organisational matters as she had held an important post until 1938 during the Nazi era. However, as far as my father was concerned, she was considered "only a widow", as the women were still trying to outdo each other with regard to their prominent husbands.

'I was the one whom my mother could "rely on". I had to play the role of a courier. I had to keep an eye on the "little ones" even though there were much older children and boys around who would have been more suitable for various jobs, and who, in addition, refused to "obey" me. However, living together in such a small space had to be organised somehow.

'I clearly recall one incident. I presume I had left the train to relieve myself and found myself alone in deep snow, about ten metres away from the train, when suddenly low-flying fighter planes approached. Everyone inside the train ducked, in order to create the impression of an empty train. A railway man and myself threw ourselves under the train. This is what we had learned to do even if it exposed us to the risk that the train might suddenly start moving.

'However, the wagon provided a measure of protection. The snow was high, but suddenly there was a spray of snow and earth from the impact of the bullets. I was lying very still and held my breath, in order not to betray myself through the air that I exhaled. The memory of this story was brought back to life when my daughter asked me one day whether I had nearly suffocated while lying in the snow. My daughter had seen such an image. The railway man was hit: a lot of red blood coloured the snow like in Snow White's story. The railway man never got up again.

'I had already seen a lot of blood during my short life. I was not terrified. I tried to get back on the train. After the fighter planes had disappeared, I recounted the incident of the man being under the train. Someone fetched a grey blanket, and the man was wrapped up in it. Then the grey blanket with the man inside was thrown against a hedge when the train started moving again. I heard later that it had not been possible to bury him because the ground was frozen. Some people inside the train had been injured during the attack. As there were no doctors, people's wounds were bandaged with underwear. The splintered window of the compartment was somehow covered. However, the icy wind still blew through.

'Our only drink was melted snow, which we sipped from our bare hands. Some soup handed out in one railway station was the only warm meal during our journey. When we stepped out of the train at Usedom, we could hardly move. Stiffly we staggered about and I stumbled and fell. We were then put up in a summer hotel, which was unheated, with large windows overlooking the Baltic Sea.'

This was the account of a woman who was five years old at the time she witnessed these horrific events. At an age when other children were going to primary school, this young girl had collected mental scars. It was not surprising that she decided to seek therapeutic support in order to help her to come to terms with what she had witnessed.

However, in 1999, when she attended one of my seminars about the psychological sequelae of childhood war trauma, she stated that her childhood refugee experiences were not the reason for her attendance at the seminar. Having detailed and vivid memories of what she had witnessed during the train journey, she felt there was no need to explore this issue further.

The story and the drama of this last train leaving Danzig [Gdansk] had a firm place in her life. That was the way it had happened. That was the way the curse of history had touched her childhood. It could not be changed. In the course of a lifetime she had learned to coexist with those memories.

It was for a different reason that she had decided to take part in the seminar. Whereas she possessed a clear, coherent and conscious access to the sequence of events from the time when the flight started, she had no conscious recollections of events prior to January 1945, as the key to this early space of experience had been lost. She had gone through life with an empty feeling due to a lack of connection to deep 'textures' of experiences, which had been woven together during the first years of her life. Whatever she knew about the first years of her life was based on second-hand information, which had been relayed to her. However, it lacked the vibrancy of her own, subjective perception and the immediacy of being rooted in her own emotional experience.

Even though this factual account may be seen as a reflection of true occurrences, the situation in the case of this woman, whom I shall call Mrs T, was even more complicated because she had doubts about whether what had been portrayed to her as 'factual' was actually a fabrication conceived by her mother.

Throughout Mrs T's life she had seen enough of her mother to conclude that her mother had a tendency to be 'economical with the truth', and that she fabricated events or cut out significant aspects from others whenever it suited her intentions. Mrs T therefore doubted whether there was any reliable knowledge about her first years of life at all.

What was undeniable, however, was a fact Mrs T shared with many members of her generation, namely, that her father had been killed in the Second World War. He died at Stalingrad when Mrs T was about three years old. When she talked about her father she talked about him as if she was referring to the invisible shell of someone placed in a very distant no man's land between reality and the surreal. Yes, she had attempted to get closer to her father by trying to search for his grave. She had even travelled to the site near Stalingrad where her father was allegedly said to have found his final resting place. However, eventually she was told that her father's remains were probably lying in a stretch of land covered by a motorway.

Evidently Mrs T had not given up hope of finding the key to access conscious memories of her early childhood. Failing for decades had not deterred her and it did not take long for me to realise how much hope she had attached to achieving a breakthrough during the course of the seminar. However, stating her goal so clearly did not make the situation any easier for me because I had no blueprint available as to how to assist Mrs T to achieve her long-held wish.

While I was acutely aware of the challenge of the task imposed on me, I did not conceal my state of ignorance. This, however, did not cause me any nervousness. Remaining calm and confident, I counted on the quiet cooperation of the ever helpful, though invisible, assistant of therapeutic work, namely, time.

The next day, during the lunch break, an image formed in my mind. While being preoccupied with looking out of the window, I saw a number of objects in my mind. I knew that this visual perception was not the result of rational thinking. The objects represented but a purely visual phenomenon, which had emerged in its own way. I was not aware that I was playing a conscious role in the emergence of this arrangement of objects in my mind. Although I did not discover a meaning to the images that appeared before my 'inner' eye, I did feel that the meaning would become clear at a later stage. Although the sight of the objects did strike me as strange, I knew intuitively that the transpired meaning would assist me in establishing connections to early experiences of the seminar participants. In a similar way to an architect, who holds a vision of a house in his mind and translates it into a real form with little effort, I translated my vision of an object sculpt by using real objects. I decided to translate my inner vision of objects into an object sculpt with the use of real objects at the next meeting, which happened to be that afternoon.

I did not need much time to place the objects in the seminar room. The complete object sculpt covered an area of several square metres. To create the object sculpt, I began by placing two white sheets of A4-sized paper next to where I was seated. On each of the sheets of paper I placed a rectangular block of wood which had a finely polished orange surface. I positioned my three toy animals, the lion, the rabbit and the small pink koala bear, somewhat away from the paper but even further away from the seminar participants, who were sitting in a U-shaped arrangement in the seminar room. The positions of the animal toys were such that they stood some distance apart from each other. Instead of looking at each other they created the impression that they were staring into the far distance. Closer towards the centre of the seminar room, and closer to the seminar participants, I put a variety of objects. I was not concerned with laying out the objects in a particularly logical or organised fashion. I simply picked up the objects – which consisted of four different books, several yellow building blocks, a few logs and a big block of wood – and placed them in a wholly disorganised way in the seminar room. However, I was not perturbed by the fact that the meaning of my object composition remained as yet enigmatic. I returned to my chair without giving any explanation.

However puzzling my activity might have appeared, it was not long before it became apparent that the sight of what I had constructed with the objects had evoked memories and touched the emotions of the seminar participants. Memories of childhood experiences, in particular those which occurred during and after the war, seemed to have been aroused and started to fill the seminar room with a certain indescribable atmosphere.

One seminar participant started by saying that the sight of the logs had reminded him of the time when he went with his father to the forests to collect firewood, as this was scarce during the post-war years. The toy rabbit also evoked memories. 'Rabbits. I only know rabbits, when they are being slaughtered,' said the seminar participant, alluding to the fact that there was no other source of meat available. Another seminar participant commented that the sight of the objects had made her 'terribly sad' without being able to pinpoint the cause for her sadness. Yet another participant described the emotional impact of the object sculpt by saying that it made her feel 'more and more heavy'.

Whatever memories and emotional responses had been triggered, it had become clear by now that the objects had, in fact, touched on deeper layers of experiences which the participants had had. Mrs T agreed with the other seminar participants that looking at the object sculpt had evoked a whole mosaic of post-war experiences. She mentioned that books were burnt out of fear of Russian soldiers. She, too, remembered the killing of rabbits and was brought face to face once again with the ideological fanaticism and harshness of her mother whose attitude towards the truth she had found incomprehensible and unacceptable.

However strange and seemingly detached from reality the object images I had perceived may have appeared initially, the object sculpt provided a very helpful stimulus towards elevating war- and post-war-related childhood memories of the seminar participants to the conscious surface.

These recollections were acutely present in the minds of the seminar participants. The objects had inspired processes of reconnection with (post-)war childhood experiences and, generally speaking, the objects had been a vital aid in bringing the participants' childhoods closer to the foreground.

This was also true with regard to Mrs T. However, it was equally obvious that no breakthrough had been achieved in accessing her memories preceding January 1945. If Mrs T was disappointed, she did not show it. I knew time would come to my aid.

When the seminar group met the next morning, Mrs T was visibly agitated. Without needing any prompting she reported that she had fallen asleep the previous evening without too much difficulty. Then, when waking up in the middle of the night, wholly unexpectedly the scene of her father had returned into her consciousness as he said a final farewell to her when leaving for the Eastern front. This scene re-emerged with a clarity and intensity as if it had happened yesterday. For the first time, and nearly fifty-seven years after this farewell scene between a barely three-year-old girl and her father, Mrs T had the profound experience of visualising her father in front of her eyes as if he was a living person.

'My father wore his military uniform with a rucksack on his back. A brass cup dangled down. On his head, I saw his steel helmet,' she said, continuing, 'It was dark in the corridor. My mother wore a white night dress. My father looked at me saying: "From now on you are my big girl, I am relying on you. Take good care of your mother and stand in for me because I cannot look after her now. And also look after the little child that is coming soon."'

'Then my father turned towards my mother, saying: "Take good care of yourself, my little one." These were the exact words my father used,' Mrs T concluded, adding 'my little one' was the form of address used by her father to her mother in letters from the front line. After her father had left, Mrs T remembered having packed her doll's pram. She then went to the balcony proclaiming that her little sibling 'could now come' into the world.

Overwhelmed by what she had experienced during the night, Mrs T said that she had not been aware that such a farewell scene had taken place. The imagery of the scene, the words said, the intensity of the atmosphere, everything had re-emerged and become alive again. Beyond the rediscovery of the farewell scene, she felt a new sense of closeness to her father. She described how the positive relationship she had had with him during her childhood gained a new lease of life.

Also she had suddenly become aware of her father's fateful instruction to care for her mother, whose negative implications had overshadowed Mrs T's life. Without having been conscious of the impact of her father's instruction she had obeyed it and carried it out without questioning it. For thirty years Mrs T had cared for her paralysed mother, with her mother never expressing a word of gratitude for Mrs T's self-sacrificing attitude. The relief from the pressure of this mental burden improved her physical state. Although having suffered from chronic back pains she now enjoyed an upright posture and pain-free gait.

It was as if there had been the crumbling of a hidden wall that had prevented Mrs T's consciousness from accessing her childhood prior to the age of five years. Mrs T was filled with a sense of surprise and amazement as a result of this.

Enriched by what she described in German as an *Urerlebnis*, i.e. a profound or archaic experience, Mrs T returned home at the end of the seminar in a cheerful and happy mood.

I offered Mrs T the opportunity to have a further consultation with me, which was the norm after seminars like this. Often I have observed that the remaking of links to childhood experiences that have been buried for a long time may bring further associated insights to the surface of conscious awareness. Sometimes, and particularly if early experiences have been repressed by anxieties, denials or taboos, the new insights may surge into consciousness in a vivid and intense manner.

In Mrs T's own words, it appeared to her as if a dam had been removed from a stream of water. Now an endless flow of memories flooded the landscape of her consciousness over the following two weeks. She rediscovered joyful memories relating to her father before he left, which made her feel as if she found herself on an island of bliss.

Despite her initial resistance against the forces which swept through her mind, she was gradually compelled to realise that she had witnessed more than she might have thought imaginable. Even though she had only been a small child, she had witnessed the separation and then loss of her father. She had witnessed the trembling of her mother during nightly bombing raids. She had seen bodies that had been mowed down, and she had witnessed the flight which had remained engraved in her memory with such vividness.

Slowly but surely she arrived at a point where she had no choice other than to recognise that she had witnessed even more terrible events, which had been deeply buried in the emotional substrate of her mind. Somehow she had instinctively known about them all her life without knowing how or why.

As a fanatical supporter of the Nazi regime, her grandfather had access to the concentration camp at Stutthof, close to Danzig [Gdansk]. He was the owner of a large dog and, carrying a riding whip, he would enter the camp with the purpose of selecting what he called in his contemptuous language *Arbeitstiere*, a term that in its literal translation of 'work animals' referred to imprisoned humans forced to work.

Utterly heartless towards the suffering that lay before his eyes, he was also completely unaware of the psychological impact of taking his little granddaughter to the concentration camp. Now, nearly sixty years later, Mrs T re-enters the camp in her mind. She is overwhelmed by a stream of images. At times she would break out in a cold sweat; at other times she would tremble all over. She would feel cold in the midst of the summer heat, tormented by painful restless images of terror, which would break into her conscious mind. As if it had happened yesterday, emaciated figures would line up in front of her eyes. Again she witnesses the scene of military personnel using camp prisoners as live shooting targets. Again she sees in front of her eyes 'the dark, acid floor in the chemical factory', whose shiny surface prisoners try to avoid. 'Suddenly, however,' she writes, 'there was the terrifying view of human bodies floating in the tubs filled with acid ... My thoughts come to a halt due to these frightful visions,' she stated.

'After so many decades my body still struggles. Today I experience everything from feeling sick to pains in the heart,' she continues. Even the sight of mountains of bones comes back to her memory, and she explains that throughout her life it has been impossible for her to tolerate soap. She wonders how it will be possible for her to find a forgiving end, referring to the never-ending scream from her childhood.

Once more, the forces of the images arising from her childhood overpower her. As though the devil himself were after her, she races across the compounds of the chemical factory, passing by the sheds until she collapses, feeling completely out of breath.

It takes some time before she experiences a sense of calmness and even a feeling of peace in which the scream from her childhood becomes weaker, nearly sixty years after witnessing the terrifying events, the demon of war and the evil of genocide. A few days later she writes: 'I no longer want to say to myself "I don't want to live anymore." Now, at last, I want to live. I am now singing and it makes the scream fade away.'

CHAPTER 4

RECOGNISING PATTERNS

*Most of the war years I spent in Munich, par hasard plutôt, waiting, always thinking
the war must take an end, not understanding, not understanding, not understanding.
Not understanding, indeed, was my main preoccupation throughout these years. I
assure you this was far from easy!*

Rainer Maria Rilke, letter to Leopold von Schlözer, January 1920

(POST-)WAR CHILDHOOD TRAUMA.
THE MOSAIC OF PSYCHOLOGICAL SEQUELAE

The observations I have described in the previous chapters represent only a
fraction of a much broader spectrum of late psychological manifestations arising
from (post-)war trauma suffered in childhood. Pursuing what looked at first sight
to be inconspicuous pointers or little more than hunches guided me towards
unexpected phenomena and discoveries relating to childhood war trauma.
Sometimes I applied a small dose of common sense or deductive thinking; mostly,
though, the results were not achieved by following the pathways of particular
psychotherapeutic schools of thought but by circumventing the workings of my
conscious logical mind.

The awareness of a whole spectrum of psychological manifestations due to childhood (post-)war trauma developed and I was filled with a growing sense of certainty that the phenomena which I had observed over the years with my own eyes and discovered were, indeed, real. The complex mosaic of phenomena I observed never ceased to amaze me.

Again I see a woman standing in front of me, in the centre of a seminar room. Her professional competence had enabled her to rise to the top of her profession in the field of academic teaching. In the dimly lit seminar room, during the evening session, something seemed to have happened to this woman, as her confident and self-assured manner dissolved into a helpless, silent shyness. Standing a couple of metres away from me she was motionless and lost for words. She could not find any words to communicate with me. Simultaneously, I was paralysed in my communication with her as I failed to initiate a conversation. For about half an hour we became two people who were unable to communicate and break through a barrier of silence.

Sometimes we, the wordless bodies, moved a step closer and then moved further apart, until I suddenly felt the impulse to take off my wristwatch. Without having any idea of why I was doing this, I took off my wristwatch slowly and cautiously placed it to her ears so that she could hear its ticking noise.

Immediately her timidity disappeared, allowing her to find the words to tell me about her childhood war experiences. She began by saying that her father had been a soldier during the Second World War and subsequently a prisoner of war. She grew up with her father being absent. She was four years old when, for the first time in her life, she met the man who happened to be her father. To her, her father was a stranger and at that time the little girl was scared of the stranger and overcome by fear. Only when her father pulled out his beautiful watch from his pocket to show it to her did the strangeness break down between them.

Again, a man who was born in a town in Poland stands in front of me. He told me that he was only two years old when his mother was forced to flee Poland with him — a story whose beginning reminded me of many similar stories that I had listened to over the years.

On this particular occasion, I was struck by this man's slow manner of speaking. It was not just the slow way in which he spoke that caught my attention; I also spotted the fact that he made frequent pauses between words and sentences. I had to wait a long time for him to complete a sentence, and sometimes even for individual words to emerge from his lips.

From my observations, I asked him about the duration of his fleeing from Poland to Germany. Again, I had to be patient while I waited for an answer. Eventually he told me that he believed the flight had 'not taken a long time'. I had no reason to doubt the sincerity of this answer, but curiosity drove me to ask him once more whether he was able to define the duration of the flight more accurately.

'I presume the flight must have taken more than two days. Maybe two weeks?', I asked him. Again his reply came slowly and, again, he remained vague in his definition of the time it had taken. This, however, fuelled my curiosity and the desire to obtain exact information from him even more. Persisting in my questioning until the full truth came to light, he finally told me that the duration of their flight had amounted to two years.

However, this was not the end of the story, as he told me that it took at least the same amount of time for his family finally to settle into a village in West Germany. Many years have passed since his odyssey as a refugee child. He now lives in his own house, but in order to prevent himself from ever feeling cold again he had not one but two independent heating systems installed in his home. In order to avoid ever being exposed to starvation again, he fitted a very big larder in his house. This is always filled up with an ample supply of food.

Again, I see another man standing in front of me. He is tall and his stiff upright posture makes him even taller. The man had attended the seminar because he wanted to examine unresolved issues relating to his war childhood. Of course, I was prepared to work with him. However, unexpectedly I felt a sudden urge of not wanting to work. I was certain that this was neither due to laziness nor to the late hour of the day. I was filled by this overwhelming wish to spend my time playing with balloons. I began to throw a balloon in the air and then towards the man, thinking it would be fun for him to join in playing as well.

The man, however, did not respond and continued to stand still and erect like a candle. Yet, despite his stiff, upright posture he looked helpless, possibly because he did not know what to make of a seminar leader who should have engaged in some proper serious work with him, but who, instead, had chosen to indulge in enjoying himself by playing childish balloon games.

Sadness descended upon the man as he became more aware of what a terribly serious affair the war had been. He told me that there had been nobody to play with him during his childhood. His father was far away in a distant land, fighting in the war, and his mother had been preoccupied with survival. Throughout his life nobody had ever perceived the burning desire within him to play, one of life's most beautiful, profound and simple gifts.

On another occasion I see a man in front of me with a strong physique like that of a woodcutter. However, instead of sitting in a chair during the sessions, like all the other seminar participants did, he displayed a somewhat puzzling behaviour.

For no obvious reason he often got up in the middle of a session and walked away. Then, maybe hours later, he simply returned, entering the seminar room as if nothing had happened and as if this was a very natural way to behave. I gained the impression that this was not done in order to irritate others, but that he was simply doing what he felt appropriate. My first hunch was that he behaved as if everything around him, including himself, was in constant movement. If this hunch was anything to go by, then the question I was asking myself was: What was the link between this man's behaviour and his life story?

It did not take long for a story of a refugee to emerge once again. For two whole years he and his large family were pushed around by the 'waves of war'. They drifted across central Europe forwards and backwards. They lived like 'gypsies' in a covered wagon, which was their home and which was always on the move.

It appeared that the constant drifting and travelling had shaped his mind and behaviour to make him feel as if he was always on the move. Further evidence for this hypothesis came to light when he told me about his school years after the family finally settled down and sent him to school. He had often been told off for getting up in the middle of a lesson. He would wander around as if the wheels of his earlier life 'on the road' as a refugee were still turning during his school days, in the same way as they were now in the seminar room.

On another occasion I saw a woman in front of me who appeared to be affected by restlessness. This made it impossible for her to sit still on a chair. Her hands and her legs moved constantly and the pronunciation of her words was so blurred that I had difficulties in understanding her. She was a medical colleague and she confirmed that she had no involvement with drugs and no neurological damage that could have accounted for her restlessness. As a result, at this point in time I could not understand the nature of her behaviour.

Finally, I wanted to see her walk around the seminar room in order to have a closer look at her gait, although at that moment I did not know why this should be relevant. I was aware that asking her to 'parade' in front of the other participants might be considered a somewhat odd request, but it was important for me to try to understand her behavioural problem. She agreed and I could now observe her walking round the seminar room. Still wondering what I was intending to observe, I became aware that her body movements reminded me of those of a wooden doll. When she walked there appeared to be a poor coordination of her limbs, resulting in a lack of smooth and continuous 'flow' of her body movements. The clumsy pattern of her movements made me suddenly wonder whether, at some stage in her early life, there may have been a disruption of the normal development of gait, thus preventing a smooth and rhythmic integration and harmonious interplay of body movements. Even though this was an attractive idea, it remained nothing more than that until an answer could be found to the question of what could have been responsible for such a disruption in her movements.

Soon an answer emerged. Born in East Prussia, the woman was barely a few weeks old when she found herself thrown into the role of a refugee baby. Heading westwards in unheated trains, she was fighting to survive through the remorseless cold winter. The flight lasted half a year and during this time she fell seriously ill and became emaciated.

Never having previously made a link between the flight and the pattern of her walking, she now remembered that the onset of her walking was delayed and characterised by clumsiness. This conscious awareness seemed to help her to regain a more normal pattern of movement in subsequent years. In addition, the restlessness virtually disappeared once it had become clear that it was due to surges of anxiety, especially when she was in new places and felt disorientated. This was another legacy of the early traumatic flight with its constant anxiety-provoking changes of location.

I recall another woman who had come to see me. She spoke about her father not having lived up to the role of a real father in her eyes. The man who returned home after the war was the biological shell of a father, whose mind and spirit had been darkened by the war years and captivity. After coming home, he suffered from depression for years. His life melted away while he was lying on his bed.

Only now, as an adult woman, my patient could break her silence of how her father had treated and affected her. One day, when she was in the kitchen, at a time when she was about to leave home, her father had tried to rape her.

Imprinted in my memory is the story of another individual, a successful businessman. When he was a child he gave his father a yellow bird as a goodbye present when his father had to return to the front line. He, the child, was hoping to protect his father from the darkness of history by giving this loving present. Yet his wish was to remain unfulfilled. He was never to see his father nor the yellow bird again. As he told me his story, now at an age where he would have been older than his father at the time of war, pain covered his face, as if time had stood still with a broken heart.

Yet again I see another man who is excited while he says how, just recently and for the first time in his life, he has finally been able to break the taboo of silence by talking with his mother about the death of his father killed in action in the former Soviet Union. Seeing photos of his father's grave for the first time, the man, only in his forties, is already much older than his father was when he met his senseless death on a distant battlefield.

Now I see a woman, who described to me in simple words how the war had affected her father: 'The war has transformed my father into wood.' What she expressed metaphorically was that the war had frozen the emotional sensibility of her father, leaving her without a real father to relate to.

I recall seeing a female colleague who had became upset after a client had told her about her rape. I failed to comprehend why this colleague's mental equilibrium had been so badly affected by what she had been told. There was little in her life to indicate the reason for having the strong reaction she felt. On first impressions, finding a link to the Second World War seemed unlikely as the colleague had been born during the post-war years. I did, however, wonder whether rape might have been a hidden agenda in her family of origin. Offering this hypothesis to her, she replied that rape would not have been a topic spoken about at home. Furthermore, although her mother had been a refugee, she had not, to her knowledge, been raped.

There appeared to be no obvious answer and I would not have pursued things any further had it not been for my feeling that it would be helpful for my colleague to ask her mother in some more detail about the issue of rape. I felt it would be important definitely to exclude rape as an issue in her mother's life. My colleague accepted my advice and told me a few days later that her mother had confirmed to her that she had not been raped.

However, her mother told her that, while fleeing in the company of several female relatives, she and the other women came very close to being raped and were lucky to escape. Hearing this news for the first time from her mother had a calming effect on my colleague. Regaining her composure she quickly became her former self again.

On another occasion I see a man in front of me. He appeared distinct due to his absent-minded stare and rigid corpse-like posture. His home, like many other houses during the war, had been bombed during an air raid. Having stayed at the home during the attack, he was presumed dead like many children who perished in the ruins of their homes during the Second World War. Some time passed until it was discovered that he had survived. He was fortunately dragged out from what had nearly become an early tomb.

Once more I see a woman before me, her face reflecting the commotion of painful emotions embodied within her. She was torn between having a deep-seated anxiety regarding men and a longing for a fulfilling partnership and parenthood. Now, for the first time, she had grasped the link between her anxieties – especially her fear of her father's unpredictable outbursts of rage, which culminated in a scene when her father 'nearly killed' her brother. Now she could understand the cause for her father's behaviour. The violent eruptions of rage were the remainders of the brutality of war which had hardened her father's soft heart in the wastelands of battlefields and Siberian camps, and which had destroyed the happiness of his best years.

The image of a scene comes back to me where I see a man sitting before me in the half-lit evening seminar. He looked at me quietly while I was pursuing my vision of building a little town with wooden blocks. Eventually, like a child, I lost interest in what I had built. Realising my dreams first, my attention now turned towards dismantling what I had created. First I overturned the little houses, followed by the tower. Then I suddenly felt the desire to place candles between the 'ruins' of the former little town. Slowly I lit the candles, one by one.

The man who silently followed the rise and fall of the town had still not said a word. He sat motionless, as if time had lost its heartbeat, and he took a long time before he began to speak. The scene that I had created had reminded him of the night when, at ten years old, he walked through his home town after an air raid. 'It was like walking through hell,' he remembered, 'I shall never forget it.'

Again, I see a woman sitting before me, overcome by an anxiety which makes her body tremble like a leaf. It seemed hard to believe what she said, yet, I thought to myself: do I have the right to dismiss it?

For the first time in her life, she realised what it must have been like for her to be exposed to air raids – not as a teenager, not as a child, not as a baby, but as an unborn child in her mother's womb. At the time, when her mother was pregnant with her, her mother spent night after night rushing down the stairs to seek refuge in air raid shelters.

Next, I recall a young woman sitting before me who sought my advice. She seemed affected by a minor conflict which broke out between parents in a kindergarten school. Surely this issue had no connection to the war and, when I asked the woman to fill me in on the background, she began her account by explaining to me that 'front lines' had been drawn between opposing groups of parents. They had 'dug' themselves in the 'trenches' of their respective 'positions'. They were now 'throwing' and, indeed, 'shooting' arguments at each other. A real 'battle', she went on saying, might erupt before long because one side was preparing 'to move on the offensive'.

Normally I have no difficulties in concentrating, but this time proved different. When the woman had finished her account I had no clear recollection of what she had told me. My mind seemed to have been distracted by something which prevented me from absorbing the account she had just given to me. I apologised and asked her to describe the conflict to me once more.

Only when I listened a second time did I realise that my thoughts had been struck by the discrepancy between the harmless nature of the conflict and the use of words, which appeared to be borrowed from a military textbook.

Of course, this may simply have been a matter of linguistic style. However, I asked only a few questions before she revealed that her father had been an officer attached to the Chief of Staff of the German armed forces and had therefore been working in the headquarters of a military might which had unleashed its dominant power over the European continent. Only a short while ago the theme of the Second World War had seemed far removed from the issue of a minor kindergarten conflict, but now the iron fist of the supreme commander of the German war machine had suddenly stepped forward into the seminar room. The tentacles of war trauma stretched right into the present.

Again and again new facets of war trauma in childhood emerged in front of my eyes. The armoury of war had been silent since 1945, but the psychological wounds had not healed. The wide spectrum of wounds has lost nothing of its bewildering variations and complexities.

THE SPECTRUM OF POLYTRAUMA

For years I tried in vain to bring a degree of order into the bewildering spectrum and awesome complexity of childhood (post-)war trauma. Each individual had experienced his or her own set of exposure to trauma and an often cruel and tragic story. Volumes of books could have been filled with the stories of children who had suffered more in their short lives than many adults during their whole lifespan.

Looking, for instance, at the story of the young girl, described in 'The Silence of the Guitar' in Chapter 1, I was left with a heartbreaking list of traumas, symbolising the 'developmental milestones' of a war child's 'curriculum vitae'.

This young girl had suffered the violent death of beloved key family members such as her father, grandfather and the loss of two siblings. She had lost her family home and her country of birth. She had experienced exposure to a life-threatening illness, to cold and starvation. She had been separated from her mother while fleeing alone across a war-torn country. She had to cope with her mother's war-induced nervous breakdown and the loss of educational opportunities.

In my article 'Visual Geneogram Work and Change: A Single Case Study' (Heinl, 1987b) I have sketched out the early life of a woman who acquired refugee status while still a baby. Accompanied by her mother and siblings she endured fleeing across the Baltic Sea in the middle of an icy winter while her father was fighting at the front. However, for her, the refugee baby, the end of the Second World War meant the beginning of worse to come when she and her family were forced to spend several years in a Danish internment camp. There was neither warmth nor lightheartedness. Even a teddy bear, which might have given her some comfort and company, was unobtainable behind the fences of the camp. Instead, the sheer quest for survival was the leitmotif of her early childhood.

Taking guidance from the figure of twelve million refugees from former German settlements in Eastern Europe, of whom only about nine million survived, there must have been tens of thousands and, indeed, hundreds of thousands of children who experienced misery at a scale more reminiscent of horror films than of the modern ideal of a loving, warm and sheltered upbringing in peace.

How would it be possible to draw some more general conclusions from such shattering stories? It is often difficult to see the wood from the trees and it took me time to recognise one particular and obvious aspect of childhood war trauma, an aspect that is amply illustrated by the two stories above and by virtually all the case histories reported in this book. Usually I did not find a single definable war trauma but a network of causally related traumas or a cluster of coinciding, concomitant or sequentially occurring traumas. In fact, I was not just dealing with single traumas but, usually, with a spectrum of polytrauma.

I realised that the range of polytrauma did not only encompass purely psychological traumas such as loss, separation or witnessing brutality and destruction. Primarily physical detriments such as exposure to cold and lack of food or starvation also had to be included, as they had also left psychological scars. The childhood (post-)war trauma had not simply faded away nor had the (post-)war children simply 'grown out' of them. Quite the contrary, the polytrauma had remained virulent even after the passage of decades.

This was noteworthy from a phenomenological perspective, but also from a mental health point of view because such (post-)war traumas continued to affect adults adversely long after the official end of the Second World War. Furthermore, I realised that it was not sufficient to look at the spectrum of polytrauma in isolation, but to bear in mind that they were affecting children at different stages of their psychological and psychomotor development. Polytrauma therefore had to be seen against the background of children's development; a point to which I shall return later.

There was a wide range in terms of the time patterns of traumas. There were acute, short-lasting and chronic traumas. There were traumas such as exposure to air raids, which occurred in a repetitive manner, often at different times and with different frequency. Even if there appears to have been only a single trauma, the possibility of associated repercussions has to be borne in mind, requiring careful exploration of possible 'chain reactions' of associated secondary traumas.

The war-related absence of a father of an East Prussian family constituted, to all intents and purposes, 'only' one trauma or, at least, a stress factor, as this left his wife without a protector and stranded, having to carry the sole burden of parental responsibility for her two teenage sons. When the Soviet army advanced she felt unable to face the violence which was closing in on her, her family and community. She therefore instructed her elder son to shoot her, the mother, first, then to kill his younger brother and, lastly, to shoot himself. The son obeyed. A whole family was wiped out, one of many which were to vanish as 'civilian casualties' between the lines of military history text books.

Collective catastrophes tend to shift the axis of normality and to distort the measuring stick of perception of what constitutes a trauma. I sometimes came to observe that (post-)war trauma appeared hidden behind smokescreens of denials of suffering because it appeared normal that people had been killed, or because the fact of survival was seen to compensate for any suffering, or because the suffering was considered to be minor compared to that of others.

The woman in 'A Timeless Night' in Chapter 1 had every reason to consider herself lucky to have escaped alive. After all, about three million German refugees from former Eastern settlements perished seeking to escape westwards. The mere fact of survival, however, does not convey the whole picture. Apart from the hazards of the flight, the arrival in the West hardly amounted to a warm reception. Refugees were put up in overcrowded accommodation and, occasionally, in primitive refugee camps, some of which were operational until 1948. At that time, for instance, there were about seven refugee camps around the town of Hanover. 'Ten per cent of the refugees have no bed and sleep on the floor,' states the laconic subtitle under one photograph in Hauschild and Umbehr's (1985) book. The harsh conditions in such camps are reflected on the children's sad, miserable and sometimes disturbingly aged faces, by their insufficient clothing and lack of privacy.

The mountain of psychological problems arising from the uprooting, which in today's terms might be described as 'ethnic cleansing', was compounded by the challenge of having to adapt to a new and unfamiliar environment, even if this lay within the boundaries of the German-speaking world. In the spring of 1948 the population of Niedersachsen, one of the German federal states, consisted of thirty percent refugees (Hauschild and Umbehr, 1985). There were flare-ups of resentment by the local population against the incoming flood of 'alien' Germans from the East. A frosty welcome would only add salt to the psychological wounds of displacement, further complicating the process of growing roots in the new environment.

I learnt that the term '(post-)war childhood' trauma does not only apply to those children who were unfortunate enough to grow up in countries directly affected by the war. Even in a European country like Switzerland, which kept a prudent neutrality, children were affected by the indirect effects of the dark war clouds moving across a whole continent.

Born in 1940 in Switzerland, a colleague told me that he grew up under a 'bell of angst'. This was fed by the sense of apprehension and fear prevailing in Switzerland at the time that the country might be overrun by the German army and drawn into the maelstrom of the war. There were even more tangible repercussions for Swiss children. Many of them experienced long separations from their fathers because they were posted to watch the Swiss borders during the war.

Amongst the spectrum of (post-)war trauma, losses assume a prominent and sad place. There is the acute trauma of loss associated with the psychological reaction of mourning – provided the child was old enough to comprehend the loss and to experience a process of mourning. A father who went missing often complicated the proper mourning process by delaying it for years or even decades, creating a situation of chronic, unresolved mourning.

In both situations the trauma consisted of losing someone to whom there had been an emotional attachment. However, particularly when losing a parent, the traumatic impact of the loss did not just represent a single event but the loss of a key developmental psychological structure. The loss of a loving father, for instance, robbed the child of a parent who would have been able to provide this structuring influence by guiding and facilitating the emotional flourishing, and the intellectual and personality growth of the developing child.

Seen in this light the apparently single traumatic loss has to be regarded, in effect, as a chronic trauma removing an important developmental catalyst from the child's environment and thus jeopardising, weakening and undermining the building of the architecture of a child's prosperous personality and future.

How happy was the woman in 'A Journey into the Abyss of Consciousness: The Story of a Child Witness' in Chapter 3 to have at least regained a glimpse of her father, whom she had lost so early on and whom she would have needed so desperately for her development.

Barbara Meter (1996), in her intensely moving epilogue to a collection of letters written to her by her father from the Russian front, describes how much she yearned to have him back. Her father, a pacifist, had been drafted into the German army against his will. He took the courageous decision of shooting into the air rather than pointing his gun at the so-called Soviet enemy. Paying a high price for his lonely pacifist and eminently human stance, he was eventually executed.

Growing up without a male role model, and being raised in a 'men-free' environment, a woman explained how the absence of her father and of most men in her village deprived her of the crucial social learning experience of meeting and familiarising herself with members of the opposite sex during the formative years of her childhood and youth. She needed years to find out 'who men really were'. The difficulties of relating to members of the opposite sex had been a direct consequence of the Second World War.

Often the loss of a father as a key developmental figure did not remain an isolated traumatic event, but triggered a domino effect of further, significant secondary traumatic consequences for children by worsening the psychological climate of their living environment and thus affecting their development.

The mounting psychological pressure on the mother as the only remaining adult provider for the family usually undermined the emotional resources of the mother. The spiral of stress and strain would reduce the time, energy and quality of care needed for the child and would diminish the expression of loving mother-child interactions. Even worse, there would often be a reversal of roles. In order to compensate for the pressure on the mother, the children would, quite frequently, find themselves pushed into adult-like roles of having to feel responsible for their mothers. Burdens of responsibility were heaped on them that were wholly inappropriate, given their age, and were too heavy for their small shoulders.

Small boys were forced into the roles of grown-up men in order to replace fathers. Only three years old, a seminar participant was forced to take on the burden of his father's role. While his father struggled to survive on the battlefield, the little son was already counting the number of times he had escaped death on the 'home front'. In some cases, the little boys had to assume husband-like roles of providing support and comfort for their mothers.

Likewise little girls were pushed into the role of adult women having to assist their mothers in the task of being care providers during times of mayhem. Such pressures were not just brought to bear on teenagers or older children, but on young children too. Age offered no shield of protection.

The shock waves of a devastating and widespread 'wipeout of fathers' in one generation would be felt in the next generation. The trauma of losses is not limited to one generation but 'spills over' into the next one, displaying a transgenerational effect. The fatherless children will eventually grow into adults, yet deep in their hearts they may have remained children who continue to yearn for the fathers they never had. Instead of being able to provide a grounded father model for their own children, they search for being fathered themselves. The unresolved grief for the lack of a fatherly role model was, for instance, the key issue in the case of the man who was overcome by sudden sadness during the play with the balloons. Similarly, this was an issue in the men in 'A Mourning Ritual' and 'The Silver Necklace' in Chapters 1 and 3 respectively.

The extent of war losses in families can become quickly visible on drawings of geneograms, a technique which involves the sketching of family trees over three or more generations. Invariably, the visual display of the geneogram will highlight the scale of the losses of family members during the Second World War, but also during the First World War. More than once, while looking at geneograms and counting the number of crosses indicating family members killed during these wars, I felt as if I was walking across a war cemetery.

The staggering loss of millions of fathers during the Second World War produced many orphans. Yet there is another disturbing war-related issue which is underrated, although it appears to me of great significance. This is the issue which I define as 'emotional fatherlessness'. What I am referring to, are fathers who survived but who were so badly damaged psychologically by the experience of war and the prisoner of war years that they were rendered unable to fulfil a father's role in a way which would have been beneficial to their children. In a nutshell: these fathers were alive but were unable to provide a healthy psychological growth structure for their children. Lehmann's (1986) study on German long-term prisoners of war in the former Soviet Union illustrates the scale of the psychological damage. More recently Shay's (1994) book *Achilles in Vietnam. Combat Trauma and the Undoing of Character*, provides a frightening insight into the magnitude of psychological destruction as it affected former US Vietnam veterans.

One of the fathers I referred to in '(Post-)war Childhood Trauma: The Mosaic of Psychological Sequelae' illustrates the concept of emotional fatherlessness. When he returned home from the battlefields he suffered from depression for many years after and was unable to offer his daughter a role model that would sufficiently facilitate her emotional growth. Eventually he attempted to rape her.

In the words of another woman, the war had transformed her father 'into wood'. This left the woman, his daughter, without the lively presence of an emotional father model. The father of yet another woman had turned to drinking and into an emotional wreck. Despite decades having passed, he was still unable to talk in a coherent manner about what must have been unimaginable horrors. Still held captive by the relentless grip of these unresolved traumatic experiences, he was incapable of offering his daughter the psychological structure she would have required.

Even though the number of mothers who were killed during the Second World War was much smaller than that of fathers, there were children who lost their mothers, or indeed both parents, during the course of the war.

Bearing in mind the existential situation of mothers during the Second World War, it is evident that their reduced scope of attending to the emotional and developmental needs of their children affected the children adversely. Applying the working concept of 'emotional fatherlessness' to mothers, I should like to suggest the notion of 'emotional motherlessness' in order to draw attention to the emotional deprivation experienced by children as a result. Whether the mothers suffered traumas as a result of losing their partners, as a result of having been raped, as a result of losing their homes and familiar social ambience, or of losing their careers, the repercussions of those traumas for their children may have been of such a magnitude as to leave their children without the emotional care and loving attention they would have required. The mother of the man in 'The Memory of a River Crossing' in Chapter 1 illustrates this very point.

Apart from the great number of children who had lost one or two parents, and who had to bear the brunt of transgenerational war damage, there are countless numbers of children who grew up in a psychological environment of emotional fatherlessness and/or motherlessness. They are part of what I call the neglected collective of emotional orphans.

Although these children have had a surviving parent or parents, it was only their parents' body shell that had stayed alive because their former soul had been swept away by the bloody tide of war. What had remained were people with various degrees of often crippling psychological damage.

If my experience is a guideline, I should like to refer to my rule of thumb. Unless proof has been provided to the contrary, I regard anyone who has survived the war as having been traumatised in some way or other. Sadly enough, I see less and less grounds for changing this rule the longer I work with (post-)war-traumatised individuals.

The generation of the so-called German 'Wirtschaftswunderkinder', i.e. children of the German economic miracle, illustrates the particular usefulness of the concept of emotional fatherlessness and motherlessness. These were children who had been born after the end of the Second World War and after the immediate post-war period, at a time when the living and material conditions had improved – at least in former West Germany.

However, the reality of their psychological environment during their upbringing cannot be properly understood without reference to their parents' war trauma. These children of the German economic miracle were born after the particularly harsh deprivations of the immediate post-war period had been overcome. They were neither war children, in the sense of having been exposed to the direct impact of war, nor were they strictly speaking post-war children, in the same way as the man in 'A Spell of Dizziness' in Chapter 1.

As the offspring of war-traumatised parents, however, they were psychologically linked to the war. Although this link was an indirect one, it was based on a transgenerational transmission of their parents' war experiences and traumas. Having to grow up as sons and daughters of parents whose minds and behaviours had been affected and shaped by the apocalypse of war, they were instilled with the disturbed emotions of a war-loaded psychological environment and were therefore exposed to the misery of emotional fatherlessness and/or motherlessness as described above. Despite the glittering attribute of having been children of the German economic miracle, like the man in 'A Mourning Ritual' or the man in 'The Silver Necklace' in Chapters 1 and 3, they were nevertheless the victims of war, suffering from second generation war trauma.

Shrewdly reflecting this theme, the *Zeitgeist* prevailing at the time coined the popular saying: 'The war had ended and then it continued, at home.' Hidden behind the façade of the emerging power house of the 'economic miracle', the phrase alluded to a psychological landscape across which broken figures shuffled around, filled with sorrows, unresolved anxieties, grief, guilt feelings and shattered hopes. Notwithstanding the merits of the 'economic miracle', there was no comparable miracle of building a framework of care for children, which would have given them the opportunity to grow up in an environment tailored to perceiving their needs and sensitivities, in order to guarantee a happy upbringing.

A few years ago I listened to the account of a woman whose experience exemplifies this very point. Born in the 1960s, she seemed close to despair when she expressed her profound unhappiness about her failure to see the brighter side of life. She suffered from being intensely preoccupied with the thought that, one day, a war might take everything away from her.

Exploring her anxiety, it emerged that both her parents had been traumatised in the course of the Second World War. She told me she would have been able to cope if her parents had talked about their war experiences.

The problem was that both her parents had virtually bombarded her with their own unresolved traumatic emotions. Long after the end of the Second World War she continued to be exposed to a barrage of anxieties unleashed by her damaged parents. Left without a protective safety net, she had no chance of nurturing a sense of peace. Only when I comforted her by calmly reassuring her, which neither of her parents had been able to do, did she become calmer.

The transgenerational transmission of war trauma demonstrates the fact that the ending of wars is not dictated by historical dates. The psychological impact of war lives on because it is transmitted across the generational boundary through the patterns of interaction and communication, adversely affecting the psychological well-being and development of the second generation. Evidence like 'The Silver Necklace' in Chapter 3 suggests that the legacy of war trauma may even cross the generational boundaries into the third generation.

During the course of a geneogram seminar, I suggested to a man to draw a geneogram on a large piece of paper in order to help him to gain a clearer view of the structure of his family of origin. In line with the instructions, he indicated the various members of his family and their mutual relationships by using a set of simple symbols such as circles, squares and lines.

When looking at the completed geneogram drawing, it emerged that his paternal grandfather had been the captain of a German submarine. Tragically he lost his life during the First World War, some seventy years earlier, when his U-boat sank. It quickly became evident that the loss of his grandfather had never been mourned properly within the family, possibly due to the fact that the man's mother had been a young girl when she lost her father.

Reflecting on how to overcome the decades of unresolved mourning, the idea of a somewhat unusual 'burial ceremony' entered my mind. Rather than talking about his grandfather with his mother, and to discuss how the loss and its unresolved mourning had affected the family, I suggested to the man to fold a little ship from paper, to put it into the bath tub at home and to let it 'sail' across the 'waves' of the 'sea' in the bath tub. Adhering to a symbolic replay of the U-boat's sinking decades earlier in lonely seas, I suggested that he should invite his mother to watch the paper ship. While the little paper ship would sink and disappear in the depth of the 'waters', there would be a ceremony which would create the opportunity to say goodbye to the father/grandfather.

Later the man told me that the ceremony had helped him to grieve the loss of his grandfather. It had also helped his mother to come to terms with the early death of her father in her childhood.

In principle the long-term consequences of a trauma also depend on the psychological resources and professional support and expertise available at the time of the incident. This general principle applies to both physical and mental health. Unfortunately, however, such options were hardly available for (post-) war-traumatised children during or after the Second World War. D. Burlingham and A. Freud's study *Young Children in War-time* (1942), in which they described the psychological effects of war on nursery children in London, was very much the exception. Similarly, the work of the educationalist L. Walz in a home for war children in Switzerland in 1945, was unusual as 'empathy and understanding ...' were leitmotifs' for her approach to war children, 'by contrast to the prevailing practice in the (war) children's homes', which was based on 'routine guarding and controlling' (Geve, 1997: 32).

It may also be helpful to bear in mind that there was a lack of professional awareness and expertise to deal with the sheer magnitude of the problem. From a public, mental health service and resources point of view probably thousands, if not tens of thousands, of properly trained mental health professionals would have been required to cater for the complex needs of scores of (post-)war-traumatised children.

Looking at the photographs of hundreds of children taken by G. Gronefeld (1985) in the Berlin of 1945 immediately after the war, or at the photographs of children in refugee camps in 1947/48 (Hauschild and Umbehr, 1985), brings home the depressing scale of unmet needs. Ironically, a whole 'army' of mental health professionals would have been necessary to undo just a fraction of the damage inflicted by the senseless actions of armies and their leaders. Unfortunately, their foresight hardly surpassed the range of their artillery when it came to consider the impact of their actions on the next generation.

Of course, it has to be borne in mind that the fields of child psychiatry and child psychotherapy were still in their infancy. Family therapy, for instance, did not exist at all and there was virtually no special expertise in dealing with (post-)

war-traumatised children. Generally speaking, the custodial approach towards war children, alluded to above, was complemented by the fact 'that early studies of children in war, tended to emphasise their resilience in the face of extreme adversity' (Smith, 1998).

Rather than fostering the creative growth of the new field of psychotherapeutic thinking, the Nazi regime in Germany had spared no effort to worship and to glorify war and its exploits. By ruthlessly forcing the intellectual and artistic elite and the greatest talents in mental health into exile it deprived war children of possible carers.

There was little on offer for the care of (post-)war-traumatised children, and I presume it is correct to say that there was virtually nothing available in terms of a standard of professional care facilities which would be considered necessary from today's point of view.

The thrust of care for (post-)war-traumatised children was therefore left in the hands of their families. Here and there, beyond the measure of providing support to survive, emotional care was offered to children. In my experience, however, and bearing in mind the impact of war on affected families and society as a whole, this has to be seen as the exception rather than the rule. After all, traumatised families, and indeed societies, are hardly able to muster the resources for a sophisticated psychological support if existential issues such as housing, clothing, food and heating are at stake. Several case illustrations in this book show the intensity of traumatisation of whole family systems, which were of a degree that simply exceeded the capacity to provide a counterbalance of emotional support. Very frequently even husbands and wives did not communicate about what they had experienced. To this day, I am being told by former (post-)war children that they regret never having been told, especially by their fathers, about their own experiences during the war. It appears that silence filled the cavities of wounds that never healed.

From the children's point of view, the lack of help offered by the professionals, the families and social environments often resulted in adding neglect to injury. This has to be viewed as an important factor in hindering the long-term recovery by, in essence, maintaining the problems. How can a broken leg heal if the fracture is not attended to speedily? Therefore, unconscious, unrecognised and untreated (post-)war-related traumas were likely to remain unresolved and to be 'dragged' through life, inhibiting the child's full growth potential.

The failure to recognise childhood (post-)war trauma is likely to leave the sufferer at the mercy of difficulties. Unresolved unconscious traumas may exert a powerful grip on an individual's mind and behaviour and are therefore prone to influence the patterns of social interactions and the shaping of an individual's life adversely. If the true origin of the difficulties – namely, (post-)war childhood trauma – has not been understood, then the individual's difficulties may be wrongly attributed to lack of willpower, weakness, or unsolvable personality problems. An individual may find himself/herself in a vicious circle of suffering, where social criticism or rejection is heaped on to the original unconscious and unresolved (post-)war trauma.

In other words, the individual may experience what I call 'double suffering' due to the fact that the continuous presence of an unrecognised, primary (post-) war trauma has attracted layers of social rejection. Insult has been added to the original injury by rejecting or even stigmatising the individual.

To complicate matters further, 'double suffering' may give rise to 'triple suffering'. While suffering from (post-)war childhood trauma, individuals concerned may not recognise the unfairness of the negative connotations expressed towards them. He/she may not comprehend that they are based on a misperception of the true nature of the problem. He or she may, in the end, absorb the negative connotations and incorporate them into his or her self-image, which may lay the seeds for negative self-belief, low self-esteem or self-rejection, and may prove hard to change. Being unaware of the unresolved (post-)war childhood trauma, and being unaware of the misperception that led to social rejection, individuals may wrongly believe that everything is their own fault.

Although there are invididuals who possess an astute awareness of the war-related nature of their psychological problems, there are many cases, even amongst professionals, where such insight is lacking or only hazy and incomplete.

This is illustrated by the story of Dr A in 'The Silver Necklace' in Chapter 3, and also in the case of a man who, in his own judgment, considered himself a weak person. His lack of assertiveness was so serious that his situation had worsened to the point where even his job was at risk. Telling me about his background, it emerged that his father, a German army officer, had been killed in action when the man was still in infancy. Within less than an hour it had become evident that the man had never been able to mourn the early loss of his father. Even more to the point was the fact that his current predicament was linked to this unresolved grief. When the man became consciously aware of his early loss, and when he obtained a more detailed mental picture of the kind of person his father had been, his psychological condition stabilised. His self-esteem rose to the extent that he resolved his difficulties at work quickly and successfully.

Whereas adults have reached a stage of relative stability in terms of personality formation, children proceed through intense and astonishing processes of development. When considering trauma in relation to children, it appears vital to pay attention to the age at which a given trauma affected the child because a given trauma may have different long-term effects, depending on the age it struck the child. A given trauma impacting the mental world of a tiny baby, of a six-year-old child, or of a fifteen-year-old adolescent, may produce rather differing long-term consequences; in other words, what may be seen by one age group as a somewhat minor trauma, such as the loss of a teddy bear, may remain a source of intense psychological pain to another age group. The inclusion of the developmental context appears to be a necessary step in order to obtain a full and coherent picture of the impact of a (post-)war trauma in childhood.

This aspect is echoed by Yule *et al.* (1999: 37) who, while reviewing previous work, state that 'it is not simply that a stressor has an effect in a simple linear fashion, but rather that the stressor interacts with the child at a particular point in development and sets in train a number of complicated reactions.' Similarly, Pynoos *et al.* (1999: 15–42) argue that 'advances in the developmental epidemiology of traumatic stress support the adoption of ... a complex developmental perspective.'

The inclusion of the developmental context helps us to better understand the long-term psychological effect of the loss of a father, for instance. As I have pointed out, the loss of a father will in all likelihood cause a traumatic experience of loss. However, by having lost a father in the war the child may also have lost a figure who might have been an important catalyst for enhancing the child's mental and physical abilities, its self-esteem, its talents and, indeed, personality. The particular risk of a trauma affecting a child therefore lies in the fact that the trauma may weaken or undermine a child's development by removing growth-enhancing structures from the external environment of the child, or by immobilising internal motivational forces.

The adult approach to the world appears to be characterised by a greater tendency to compartmentalise, such as drawing boundaries between body and soul, emotions and thinking, between will and drives, between past and future. The child's world, in contrast, carries a much more unitary flavour and, indeed, flow of interconnectivity. The developmental view of (post-)war childhood trauma is likely to lead to a greater understanding of the effects of a trauma in the interconnected world of a child.

The story of the man in 'A Spell of Dizziness' in Chapter 1 underlines this developmental view of a trauma. The exposure to cold and starvation crossed the boundaries between the bodily and the psychological domains. The psychological damage caused by malnutrition had invaded the very core of his perception of his self. Likewise, the case of the woman in the 'Mysterious Depression' in Chapter 1 shows how vital it is to bear in mind the 'dualistic' effect of traumatic exposure to cold. It was not only her body that suffered, but her mind as well.

If what I have said about traumas may sound too abstract, I would like to invite the reader to make use of his or her own eyes and to look at the pictures of children taken by the photographer Gronefeld (1985) in Berlin after the capitulation in 1945. There are scores of children whose faces show the imprints of sadness and of suffering. Given the opportunity to look at the same faces of the now grown-up (post-)war children decades later, the observer would still, undoubtedly, see traces of sadness and suffering remaining.

Reflecting on the sight of faces mirroring the misery of war, it may occur to the observer that war is a scourge that has destroyed more lives than many other plagues. The effects of this scourge continue to affect the minds and bodies of subsequent generations, as if mimicking a hereditary transmission, even more than half a century after the weapons have been laid down. However, the name of this scourge is hardly mentioned in medical, psychiatric or psychotherapeutic textbooks: it is war.

DISTURBANCES OF MENTAL ORGANISATION. ANXIETY, DEPRESSION, POST-TRAUMATIC STRESS DISORDER AND BEYOND

Childhood (post-)war-induced trauma causes a bewildering range of long-term psychological problems. Anxieties rank high in the list of long-term sequelae of (post-)war childhood trauma. Acute and chronic anxiety states and panic attacks can occur decades after the original trauma. Hearing the sounds of aeroplanes or sirens, for instance, may trigger panic attacks lurking beneath the surface of consciousness. Unresolved, simmering anxieties about one's own (post-)war childhood trauma may be mobilised by watching the news about wars taking place in other parts of the world. The unhealed wounds of anxieties dating back to adolescence, childhood, infancy and even antenatal times may unexpectedly flare up. There may be ever-present fears of future wars. Anxieties about separations or losses may be persistent and particularly notorious sequelae of early war childhood trauma, as they may interfere with an individual's ability to engage in relationships, to cope with the challenges of parental roles, new ventures or the taking on of risks. Anxieties may hinder the ability to enjoy the pleasures of life for fear that everything would be taken away by fate once more.

Barely concealed in some cases, anxieties may, in other cases, be encased in a tomb of denial in order to maintain the pretence of a well-functioning personality, strong enough to cope with anything. The story of the woman in 'Angst. The Grimace of War' in Chapter 1 reveals the intensity of emotions which were released once the anxieties became conscious after having been pushed under the floorboards of consciousness for decades.

'Tränen sind hartes Wasser', that is 'Tears are hard water' (my translation), a line from one of Gottfried Benn's famous poems, could be taken as a metaphor for the litany of depressive pictures I have seen in individuals suffering from (post-)war childhood trauma. The mountains of sadness and depression, piled up by the spades of war, rank high next to the pictures of anxiety. Again and again, the sadness of loss emerges as a towering feature. There is sadness about long and painful separations, about the senseless annihilation of loved ones. Feelings of loneliness persist, which are due to separations enforced by the ruthlessness of war. Depressive manifestations range from episodes characterised by suicidal mood swings to those where the outlook on life is tinged with melancholy.

Depressive phases may occur without apparent cause, as described in the 'Mysterious Depression' in Chapter 1, until their roots are traced back to childhood (post-)war trauma. The longing for peace, which was missing in childhood, may be so strong that death appears as the only provider of peace. The boundaries between life and death may be blurred in an individual's mindset, reminiscent of L. Walz's astute observation about war children who 'are so familiar with life and death that they do not even shy away from suicide in order to free themselves from an unpleasant situation' (quoted in Geve, 1997: 33). There are accounts where the pulse of life is only felt in the vicinity of death, because wartime experiences had inextricably linked death and life. A hectic, insatiable drive to live, may, in other instances, mask an attempt to flee the depressing memories of the furies of death witnessed in early childhood or to compensate for wasted years of war childhood and adolescence. Ever-present feelings of hopelessness and despair may fuel never-ending attempts to search for fragments of sense in a void of senselessness. Although there may be a temptation to think that half a century should have provided a sufficient time to mourn the losses, evidence suggests that in some cases the mourning has not even started.

Apart from the range of anxieties and depressive phenomena described, I have also seen occasional evidence of post-traumatic stress disorder (PTSD), such as recurrent dreams and nightmares or flashes of film-like recurrences of past horrors. The flare-up of visual reminiscences of past trauma may lead to a sudden submergence in 'black holes' which are inaccessible to language, such as is illustrated in the case of the woman in 'The Silence of the Guitar' in Chapter 1. The story of Mrs T in 'A Journey into the Abyss of Consciousness. The Story of a Child Witness' in Chapter 3 is another example suggesting persistent PTSD.

Although these pathological states which rely on psychiatric criteria are very important in terms of assessing the long-term consequences of (post-)war childhood trauma, my observations suggest that the traumatic effects cover even wider areas of the complex and intricate mental landscape. War, 'the frightening ghost of the early years of childhood' was 'to cast its shadow over the world of feelings', summarises the writer Peter Handke (2000). In this statement he describes the early forceful impact of war on his emotional life and the 'global' impact of the war on the emotional world of a developing child.

There may be a persistent sense of vulnerability, *vis-à-vis* the cruelty of war, that suffocates any comfort of peace. The power of the early (post-)war traumas may be such that their persistent mental presence may sabotage the design of a purposeful life, thus leaving the individual stranded with a sense of yearning for those precious commodities which were missing in an infant world overwhelmed by war: the innocence of peace, tranquillity and protection.

Such frames of mind are evidence that even half a century after the end of the Second World War some of those who have witnessed the deeds of war in infancy are still struggling to draw a boundary between the past and present.

Traumatic experiences may have hindered the flourishing of a sense of identity or leave behind a shattered self-esteem, particularly in refugee children or in the offspring of refugees such as Dr A in 'The Silver Necklace' in Chapter 3. A feeling of uprootedness and of having been unable to grow roots in the new 'host' environment may prevent an individual from creating a sense of feeling 'at home' within themselves. A long search, sometimes across many countries, may ensue in order to arrive at one's own individuality, or this attempt may fail.

The various stories described in this book provide intriguing evidence about the way in which the (post-)war childhood experiences infiltrated the mindsets of the individuals concerned. The story of 'An Infant's Journey' in Chapter 1 made me aware of how a horrific journey in childhood was moulded into a concept about the essence of life. It appeared that the impact of the trauma on a developing infant was not simply memorised but influenced the shaping of this child's view of the world.

Similarly, the story of the man in 'A Spell of Dizziness' in Chapter 1 suggests that there was more at work than the 'storage' of the trauma of hunger during his early childhood. Again, this traumatic episode seeped into deeper layers of his developing psyche by leaving the man with a lack of feeling emotionally saturated. This affected his capacity to form relationships and to find lasting happiness. The long-term effect of this (post-)war trauma in childhood, i.e. malnutrition, grew into more than an issue of having little to eat and of having an empty stomach. It spread across the architecture of this man's sense of self and consciousness.

As a child, the woman in the 'Mysterious Depression' in Chapter 1 experienced traumatic exposure to the cold. Again, this had rather complex consequences, as the grip of the cold was not restricted to her body, but invaded her psyche as well affecting both the physical domain and her psyche. The repercussions of this chilling experience affected her mind to the extent that she suffered recurrent episodes of depression. Furthermore, the woman was left with a vulnerability and heightened sensitivity not only to the cold but also to emotional coldness.

Although Dr A in 'The Silver Necklace' in Chapter 3 experienced no direct exposure to (post-)war childhood trauma, his case of second generation war trauma illustrates the extent to which the transgenerational transmission of trauma interfered with the development of a solid sense of identity and security.

These observations and considerations suggest that (post-)war trauma infiltrated the finely tuned and immensely complex organisation of psychological life in infancy and affected the processes of psychological development. therefore presume that the trauma produced developmental damage to the mental organisation of complex psychological concepts about the self, the relationship to others and the world in general.

Introducing the idea of developmental damage of (post-)war trauma brings into focus the effect of the trauma on the child's mental organisation and may help to perceive the wider and less visible ramifications of the damage beyond anxieties, depression and post-traumatic stress disorder.

By stating 'If intuition is a "way of knowing and learning", then like the other cognitive modes, it may have its roots in the person's early development, the initial nurturing environment in infancy', Atkinson (2000: 48–49) suggests a highly interesting link between the requirements for the development of intuitive abilities, referring to a link between the trust in one's judgment in particular, and early development.

By emphasising support, direction and structure as important ingredients of the early environment for fostering the formation and development of the ability to form judgements and intuition in general, it is easy to see that the development of such abilities will be impaired if such developmental conditions are not fulfilled. It is evident from the case descriptions I have given that, by and large, (post-)war children lacked such a nurturing environment. It is therefore plausible to conclude that (post-)war traumas are likely to have affected adversely the development of intuitive abilities due to the lack of the appropriate nurturing environment.

My own observations, in seminars designed to explore links between thinking patterns in adulthood and early childhood, provide anecdotal evidence to suggest that the nurturing deficiency of the wartime environments adversely affected the growth of intuitive abilities. Of course, these are only preliminary findings, but they do suggest the need to be aware of the possibility that the impact of war trauma strikes into the heart of the 'operating system' of mental organisation and logistics by interfering with the smooth and autonomous development of intuitive and judgmental abilities.

If the Second World War was a global war, then the considerations I have presented may suggest the disturbing thought that its traumatic effects on the world of children's minds were truly global, too.

CHAPTER 5

UNCOVERING (POST-)WAR TRAUMA IN CHILDHOOD

[W]hat a foolish bird I had been. All along the solution of the mystery of Mars orbit was in my hands, had I but looked at things correctly. Four long years had elapsed, from the time I acknowledged defeat because of that error of 8 minutes of arc, to my coming back on the problem again. In the meantime to be sure, I had gained much skill in geometry, and had invented many new mathematical methods which were to prove invaluable in the renewed Martian campaign. The final assault took two, nearly three more years. Had my circumstances been better, perhaps I would have done it more quickly, but I was ill with an infection of the gall, and busy with the Nova of 1604, and the birth of a son. Still, the real cause of the delay was my own foolishness & shortness of sight. It pains me to admit, that even when I had solved the problem, I did not recognize the problem for what it was. Thus we do progress, my dear Doctor, blunderingly, in a dream, like wise but undeveloped children!

Johannes Kepler, in a letter to D. Fabricius, 1605

I have no particular talent; I am only passionately curious.

Albert Einstein, quoted in Wickert (1972) (my translation)

CREATING AN AWARENESS

In order to facilitate the translation of the findings of this book into clinical practice, and in order for them to be of assistance to interested mental health professionals who want to sharpen their awareness and fine-tune their perception of psychological phenomena related to childhood (post-)war trauma in adults, I am outlining some practical suggestions in this chapter.

The first point I wish to make is an obvious one, the importance of which however, cannot be overstated. It refers to the general principle which is as valid in medicine as it is in mental health, namely, that a given problem or condition can only be recognised and diagnosed appropriately if the health professional in question possesses the relevant knowledge. This principle applies as much to physical conditions, such as a stroke, malaria or glaucoma, as it does to psychological ones such as depression or (post-)war-induced trauma. The probability of late manifestations of (post-)war trauma in childhood being properly diagnosed crucially depends on the professional's awareness and knowledge about this issue. Only a proper recognition will, in the end, relieve often long-term symptoms and suffering.

Taking Germany as an example, and looking at the situation dispassionately from a child's perspective, one is dealing with a country in which millions have been killed and physically and/or psychologically maimed or injured during the war. This fact alone suggests a high probability of encountering clients in psychotherapeutic practice whose lives have been affected adversely by direct or indirect (post-)war trauma in childhood.

Therefore, as far as Germany is concerned, I am suggesting that we should bear in mind (post-)war trauma as a possible cause or, at least as a contributing factor, when assessing the aetiology of a given mental and also psychosomatic problem, whatever its initial presentation may be. Although this suggestion refers to the German context, I regard it as plausible to extend it to clinical practice in any country, such as the UK, and in particular to those where there have been widespread losses and suffering during the Second World War, such as in the former Soviet Union, Poland, former Yugoslavia, Holland, China or

Japan to name but some of the countries worst affected. Similarly, and without attempting to provide an exhaustive list, countries like Vietnam, Afghanistan, Iraq, Mozambique, Angola, Sudan, and Bosnia and Kosovo should be included because of the numbers of war children involved.

My next suggestion refers to the informative value of key biographical data such as the place and date of birth. With respect to the German situation, again bearing in mind the possible application of this suggestion to other historical and national contexts, knowing the date of birth differentiates pre-war, war, post-war children and those of the German economic miracle, and provides a useful pointer towards the possible existence of direct and/or indirect childhood war trauma.

The place of birth suggests that the person may have, for instance, suffered a refugee trauma or air raids in childhood. Taking into account the dates and places of birth of the parents may, even at a very early stage of a clinical interview, quickly point to the possibility of a war-traumatised family system and, in particular, to the likelihood of indirect war trauma.

Obtaining information about an individual's biographical background is a standard procedure of psychiatric and psychotherapeutic assessments. There may sometimes be the need to probe the details of living conditions, as the initial accounts may portray too much of a rosy picture, particularly when it comes to establishing a clear picture of the early living conditions that people suffered. 'A Spell of Dizziness' in Chapter 1 illustrates this point and also highlights the fact that the ending of a war is not always followed by a rapid recovery of material circumstances – as was the case in Germany where the living conditions during the immediate (post-)war period were sometimes worse than during the war itself.

Robert Capa's (1986) moving collection of photographs illustrates the apocalyptic scenery in Berlin in 1945, and Hauschild and Umbehr's (1985) photographs reflect the realities of living conditions in German refugee camps as late as 1948. Likewise Gronefeld's (1985) touching photographs of hundreds of children in Berlin after the capitulation may help the professional to obtain a clearer perception of the reality of living conditions forced on children at the time.

In any relatively new field, the professional is likely to find him/herself on a learning curve. This requires the assimilation of knowledge from other fields such as history for instance. On various occasions I have looked after adults who had spent their childhood years in refugee camps. Assuming that this had been German refugee camps, I was surprised to be told that they and their families had been kept for several years like virtual prisoners in Danish refugee camps after their arrival in Denmark as refugees from East Prussia. One woman remembered the sadness of not being able to obtain a teddy bear in the camp because there were not any.

The need to absorb new views, or even to unlearn preconceived ideas, refers to psychological issues and thus one's own field, too. The chance finding that in one family the youngest sibling who had been born after the war seemed to be in much worse shape than the elder siblings born during the war, was the first indication to alert me to second generation war trauma via a transgenerational transmission through the parents.

The place and date of birth may sometimes provide more detailed indications as to the type of trauma encountered. Most German cities, and particularly those of industrial, economic or strategic importance, experienced sustained bombing during the war. Often targeted for years, many cities were virtually flattened causing, in Germany alone, civilian losses of 800,000 people. Many other cities like Warsaw, Belgrade, Stalingrad, Hiroshima and Nagasaki suffered appalling destruction and civil losses. In Leningrad about one million civilians perished due to the long siege by the German army.

If the place of birth of a given individual is in what was previously a German settlement in an Eastern European country, it is virtually certain that the individual concerned suffered the pandemonium of fleeing and its spectrum of associated traumas, as described in the various case histories in this book. Some country locations like villages may have been spared the direct impact of war, but this did not shield them from the destructive magnet of war, as, throughout history armies tended to rely heavily on the 'cannon fodder' of country folk. I have seen horrendous examples of loss of life, due to war, among village populations. Any person paying a visit to village cemeteries in the German countryside will see the war memorials. The staggering amount of senseless loss of life in two world wars, and beyond, lies at the forefront.

In fact, as I find it difficult to accept the notion that any geographical part of Germany or, indeed any sector of society, could have been excluded from the impact of the Second World War, I am working on the assumption that, sooner or later, war-related trauma will be discovered.

Once indications or evidence pointing to childhood (post-)war trauma have been gathered, a platform is created from which to try to establish links between the present problem of an adult individual and its possible roots in childhood war trauma, or to define childhood war trauma as an issue which has not yet been grasped as being a problem.

I am reluctant to prescribe a recipe of how to facilitate such links between current problems and early (post-)war childhood trauma. Rigid schemes always run the risk of overlooking the individual's singularity for the sake of strict adherence to an established procedure. I therefore suggest that clinicians should be guided by the principle of trying to tune in to the individual concerned and to develop the skill of finding the right kind of catalysing approach in order to enable the traumatic experiences to emerge.

The 'Silence of the Guitar' in Chapter 1 illustrates how crucial it was not to pressurise the woman into talking about her ordeal but to grant her time and space for the inner images to grow slowly into words, even if this took years. Instead of verbal exchanges, the man in 'An Infant's Journey' in Chapter 1, for instance, found a step-by-step approach helpful. First the drawing of the long refugee journey on a map helped his feelings to move closer to his experiences. Then the visual trigger of the object sculpt catalysed the process of further attaching feelings and words to his early experiences.

Looking at photographs of family members or chronicles of home villages and towns may also be a way of facilitating access to buried memories and feelings. Even now, it is still possible to suggest to individuals to contact witnesses who may provide meaningful information about the past, including lost relatives.

I gave this advice to a seminar participant who knew very little about his father who had been killed in action. Having obtained the address of one of his father's army comrades through the help of one of several German information centres, he decided to visit and interview his father's comrade, which turned out to be a very worthwhile experience for him. In another case, I suggested to a woman that she should contact a former French officer who, as a prisoner of war had been assigned to work in her family. He had looked after her and her family in a loving way while, in accordance with the irony of war, her own father was busy fighting the French. Unfortunately the woman discovered that the former French officer had already died. However, when she visited his graveside and said goodbye to him she realised that this man had been much more of a father figure to her than her own father.

I know of several cases where the love of displaced Russian women lives on in the hearts of German war children they cared for. Some of the former war children wished dearly to be able to trace their former nannies and to express their gratitude for the loving warmth they gave so generously under such harsh circumstances.

In order to allow a deeper understanding of realities, and of the psychological issues involved, I have often recommended a visit to the places of birth where the individuals themselves were born, or to places where their parents had lived before or during the war, or to trace their refugee route. I have also suggested trips to battlefield sites where fathers had spent or, to be more precise, wasted the best years of their lives. Since the fall of the Iron Curtain, and the overcoming of the absurd division of the European continent, it has become much easier to realise such plans.

Not a single stone had been left of the farmhouse in former East Prussia in which her family had lived for generations, a woman told me. Yet it had been an important experience for her to rediscover the village of her childhood, as the visit helped her to say goodbye to the past and to turn her sights towards the present and future. Unexpected surprises waited for another woman who decided to take the train into the past to revisit the site in former East Prussia where she had spent her early childhood years. She found the farm which had been the parental home and from where her family had to flee.

However, rather than being made to feel an unwelcome stranger, the current owner, a Polish farmer, received her as his guest and made every effort to extend his heartfelt hospitality towards her. Entering the bedroom the woman discovered a photograph of her family at exactly the same place where it had been left hanging when they had been forced to flee. The current owner, himself a war-displaced person, had left the photograph in its place as a sign of respect and of human dignity towards the woman's refugee family — a gesture that moved the woman profoundly.

Returning to the issue of the type of war trauma, it is important to bear in mind that childhood or adolescent war trauma also encompasses the experience of having been forced to fulfil military or quasi-military roles. Many German school children were ordered to serve as so-called 'Flakhelfer' (anti-aircraft auxiliaries). One of my clients started off in this category and was later ordered to defend an undefensible position. Not yet eighteen years old, and not even having had the opportunity to complete his secondary school curriculum, he found himself sentenced to death because he had had the courage to rescind an order by telling his little group of fellow fighters to throw away their rifles and to go home, instead of being blown into oblivion by advancing American tanks.

Bernhard Wicki's film *Die Brücke* brings home the terrible sadness of wasted youthful lives and symbolises a powerful indictment of an army command which, towards the end of the war, recruited children as young as fourteen years old.

In order to obtain a clearer picture of the transgenerational transmission of (post-)war trauma, I inquire routinely about details of the parental war history, including war injuries, illnesses contracted during the war and times spent as prisoners of war. Bearing in mind that the majority of men were in their twenties when they were drafted, and taking into account the duration of the war, some spent a total of more than ten years away from home. As the longest-serving prisoners did not return from the former Soviet Union until 1955, some men had a period of sixteen years burnt out from their lives and some only returned in order to die at home.

I tend to be sceptical when I am told that the time spent as a prisoner of wa was only 'short-lived' and therefore irrelevant, for the simple reason that at the time nobody could foresee for certain the eventual duration of the imprisonment Furthermore, conditions in some (post-)war POW camps were of such notoriety that they rendered even a short stay akin to dicing with death.

Release from captivity would certainly bring freedom, but usually not a world of bliss as a host of problems were waiting at the gates. There was the issue o the loss of loved ones or the uncertainty as to whether family members had survived. I have come across a number of cases where the loss of a fiancé had never been mourned.

There was the massive scale of war-induced injuries or ill health such as limb amputations, loss of sight, head injuries, chronic illnesses or the effects o malnutrition. There were housing problems, particularly for refugees and families who had lost their homes as a result of bombing,. There was the psychological problem of adjusting to the 'routine' of a 'normal life' after years of day-to-day struggle for survival. There were frustrations over not being able to realise the envisaged career and professional development due to missed educational and training opportunities.

It is also helpful to recognise the age at which the parents were exposed to the war. If the parents themselves were adolescents or even children at the time of the war, this may provide a potent pointer towards indirect war trauma in the second generation.

There is a photograph of advancing German infantry soldiers in Beevor'. (1998) masterly account of the battle of Stalingrad. If one were to remove the uniforms and the signs of apprehension and weariness deeply engraved in thei faces, one might be tempted to conclude that this group of very young men were on their way to a peaceful party instead of marching towards certain death.

And while these young men were shooting or being shot at, many girls o young women did not have much opportunity to enjoy the fun of life either There was loneliness, there were difficult living conditions and a constant fear o losing a loved one without even exchanging a last word or gesture of tenderness There was also mass rape, a taboo which has been carefully pushed under the rosy carpet of the 'economic miracle' by the public consciousness, rendering many women unable to enjoy sexual intimacy for the remainder of their lives. Consequently a silent burden of shattered identity and sadness, rather than joy of erotic fulfilment, was passed on to their children.

Apart from the host of problems there was the sheer insoluble, overriding moral issue of finding meaning for what had occurred after the house of cards of grandiose promises of a better world had collapsed in flames, to leave the scattered ashes of millions of victims of genocide and of war.

Obviously, expertise and confidence come from experience in dealing with the labyrinth of issues involved. However, my counsel is to look at each case as unique and always to be alert for unexpected surprises, as the devil may be hidden in the detail.

Once a woman told me that her father had become a prisoner of war in England, which did not seem in any way unusual. Continuing her account in a matter of fact style, she told me that her father had later become a prisoner of war in Poland. I had no reason to doubt the sincerity of the woman's account, and might have been prepared to let her proceed with the account of her life if I had not recognised a sudden strange feeling of something else lurking in the background regarding the story of her father.

When I asked the woman for further details, it emerged that her account had, indeed, been correct. However, an unexpected twist to the story came about when it transpired that her father had been handed over to the Polish Government by the British authorities because of suspected war crimes. He was later found guilty and sentenced to years of hard labour in Poland. Eventually released, he unleashed the full force of his sadistic personality on his family. In the case of this particular woman the main trauma was not due to the fact that her father spent years being locked away, but that he returned home to unleash his reign of terror on the family.

Uncovering (post-)war trauma in childhood depends crucially on the professional's ability to perceive the impact of the trauma from the child's point of view and not from the adult's perspective. The limited degree to which adults were capable, if at all, of perceiving the impact of (post-)war trauma in children underlines the need for more awareness. Professionals are no exception. Working with colleagues over many years I have seen numerous examples of the dimension of (post-)war trauma not having been discovered while these colleagues underwent the exploration of their own childhood, because the topic of (post-)war childhood did not form part of particular psychotherapeutic schools of training and thinking.

As I have stressed above, there has to be an awareness of the age or ages at which the child was affected by the trauma. This is crucial because one and the same trauma may have different effects at different ages. For example, a couple of weeks of separation from parents may not constitute a major problem for an adolescent. It may, however, pose a real psychological problem for a young child and may prove life-threatening for an infant.

Furthermore, there has to be an awareness of the possible developmental ramifications of a given trauma or traumas affecting a child. Rather than focusing exclusively on a particular (post-)war trauma to the exclusion of its wider impact, there has to be what can be called a sense of connectivity which allows the professional to perceive the secondary developmental implications posed by the trauma. Whereas adults have left behind the phase of their most intense developmental years, children tend to be doubly susceptible to the impact of trauma, as they are not only affected by the impact of the trauma as such, but are also highly dependent on the presence of good growth conditions. A traumatic impact on the latter is likely to have an amplifying, damaging effect. The exposure to prolonged periods of anxiety and fear may, for instance, jeopardise the development of a healthy self-esteem. This in turn may then reduce the individual's chances of successfully managing a wide range of tasks in life. Likewise, the war-induced prevention of educational opportunities may appear a comparatively minor deprivation or may not even be considered a trauma at all. However, the closure of these educational-developmental windows of opportunity may prove highly negative in the long-term.

Clearly, uncovering (post-)war trauma in childhood demands more than the correct identification of the trauma itself. It calls for tuning in with the perceptions and the mental constructs prevailing in the child's mind affected by war at the time of the impact of the trauma. This implies far more than an empathic identification with the emotional state of a given adult client in the present. What is paramount, in my view, is the professional's ability to tune in with the mental world of the child at the time of the traumatic impact. This will, of course, crucially depend on the ability to decode accurately the communicative signals transmitted by the adult individual and to 'assay' and monitor them against the internal flow of feelings and constructs as they pervaded the professional's own childhood.

There is more at stake than the sheer retrieval of facts of childhood events, and more than the precise identification of an adult's emotional state in the present. The capacity to decode relies on the professional's aptitude to connect with and 'surrender' to a child's free floating mode and grace of perceiving, sensing and thinking. This implies resisting the temptation of being restrained by views or theories about children's psychological processes which are blind to the dimension of war.

In my view, the issue of tuning into the experiential reality as perceived through the eyes of the child at the time is likely to provide the professional with a key instrument towards change, based on the principle that it is only the correct diagnosis of a problem which provides the blueprint for change. Similarly, only if the craters caused by the (post-)war trauma in the mental landscape are seen and perceived in the first instance, will it be possible to fill them.

There appears to me an analogy between the concept of good parenting and what I am outlining. If, instead of only theorising about their children's behaviour, parents tune in intuitively to the emotional kaleidoscope of their children's world, they will be successful in building bridges of communication and understanding and in fostering their children's mental growth. Obviously, in the first instance, the success of this approach will crucially depend on the parents' perception and their ability to connect freely with the wealth of experience accumulated during their own childhood. This implies, within an adult's mind, a free flow of information between the adult's and the infant's areas of experience.

Such an approach will then be successful in overcoming compartmentalisation of the world of psychological experience endemic in the adult frame of thinking and which is characterised by lines being drawn between body and soul, emotions and thinking, between will and drives, between past and future. This will enable adults to tune in with the more unitary and holistic world of interconnections in children's minds.

Uncovering (post-)war trauma in childhood does require the professional to be clear about the point of reference of what constitutes a normal environment for children. It would be unhelpful to perceive and conceive mental phenomena against the artificial definition of 'normality' as it was construed by propaganda in Germany during the war, for instance. If it was common for children to lose their fathers, then this should not be interpreted as a sign of normality.

The point of reference has to be what are considered good growth conditions from today's point of view, not notions about resilience or survival stamina. Adhering to the latter simply denies a child's fundamental right of being seen, recognised and being taken seriously in their suffering, and consequently closes the options for treatment. Inasmuch as it would never be right to state that it is normal to have a cold because virtually everybody is affected by this malaise at one time or another, it cannot be right to take the view that (post-)war trauma in childhood should be taken lightly because countless numbers of children were victims.

Modern research has shown that the formation of a well-grounded, autonomous and loving personality relies on more than pure chance. It depends on an interactive psychological framework which nurtures, promotes and catalyses a child's growth and development. The child carer's capacity to provide love and perception plays a key role in meeting a growing child's needs, a complex process in which the arts of human perception and communication work hand in hand. Such growth conditions will then feed the development, differentiation and stabilisation of psychological structures laid down in the child's mind and provide the foundations for the emergence of an autonomous self.

Viewed against such a setting of good, and indeed necessary, growth conditions for psychological development, the psychological environment offered to (post-)war children was usually lacking even the ingredients which were vitally essential. Mothers tormented by fear, anxious about their husbands' fate and constantly battling against exhaustion, were, even with the best of intentions, not in a position to offer good-quality child care, as they were unable to provide the spectrum of emotional attention and stimulating communication that would have been required to build the complex mosaic of their children's personalities.

As I have already mentioned, similar considerations apply to fathers. Spending the best years of their lives and, simultaneously, the most important years of their children's lives far away from home on the battlefields or in prisoner of war camps, such fathers were hardly in a position to nurture the growth of their children. If the infants' top requirements for growth are love, warmth, attention, perception, understanding and communication, then the wartime environment for children in a country that prides itself on being the land of writers and thinkers was wholly inappropriate as it lacked these essentials for growth. To put it bluntly, it was often simply abysmal and utterly incompatible with the notion of a modern civilisation.

An awareness of the traumatic reality of the (post-)war environment is therefore important in order to understand the broader picture and to assess the way this may have affected a given individual. However, in order to fully grasp the complexities of an individual's traumatic experiences, perception will be crucial if the traumatic long-term impact on an individual's architecture of the (un)consciousness is to be discovered – a topic that will be elaborated on in the following chapter on intuition.

If what I have tried to outline as steps towards uncovering war trauma in childhood may sound too abstract, I would like to invite the reader once more to make use of his/her own eyes and perception and to study the pictures recorded by the photographer Gronefeld (1985) in Berlin after the capitulation in 1945. There are scores of children whose faces show the marks of sadness and of suffering. At the time, their suffering was visible but not seen and there was no understanding of its long-term implications.

THE WIDER PICTURE.
OBSTACLES, CHALLENGES AND AUTHORITARIAN ABUSE

There are cases where mental health problems and their origins are correctly identified by an individual when seeking professional help and there are cases where the nature of a mental health problem is quickly pinpointed by the professional involved. Often enough, however, there are instances where the underlying cause of a given mental health problem may be lurking in such deep waters of the mind as to make a recognition far from easy. The case histories in this book provide ample illustration of such scenarios.

To uncover a childhood (post-)war trauma in an individual who is not capable of providing the relevant information poses a particular challenge to the skills of a professional.

Of course, having to gain insight into conditions whose causes are not immediately visible and recognisable is not a rare problem in medical practice. Although taking a history of the condition may provide useful and, in some cases, even decisive evidence for the diagnosis, there are sufficient examples where neither the sufferer nor the physician have immediate insight into the underlying causes, such as in head or abdominal pains. However, a whole range of technical instruments are at the medical specialist's disposal in order to advance his/her understanding of the condition's underlying cause by obtaining visual images of the underlying structures hidden from the the sight of the naked eye.

The mental health practitioner, however, does not have any such advanced technology available to assist him/her in accessing unconsciously stored information and operating mechanisms. There is little else to fall back on to cope with this tricky task. Therefore he or she has to make as effective use as possible of observational and intuitive powers in order to bring such unconscious material into the 'fluorescent' light of the conscious mind.

Like finding a needle in a haystack, one of the key challenges in this process consists of 'breaking' the hidden operational code of unconscious mechanisms by 'screening' verbal, but above all non-verbal, information and behaviour for any indication of traumatically loaded content.

Again, unlike in medicine, there is no high-tech instrument at hand to facilitate such a 'screening' procedure. While there are various psychotherapeutic approaches available due to the uniqueness of each individual's experiential world, there is very little alternative but to maximise the efficiency of the information processing powers of 'brain technology', based on crucial faculties such as sensitivity of perception and intuition whose workings are still somewhat ill-understood and which I shall refer to at a later stage in more detail.

This, however, is by no means the only problem facing the mental health practitioner when it comes to deciphering (post-)war childhood trauma. During the course of my observations on the subject, I became aware of the role of wider social influences. I came to realise that they may pose significant obstacles if they present themselves as preconceived notions, taboos or simply ignorance about issues of childhood, emotions and psychological war trauma. It appears important to me that mental health practitioners are aware of such social influences and, if needed, should be prepared to face them head-on. Their influences may, even now, block the way towards an unbiased awareness of the gruesome dimension and legacy of childhood (post-)war trauma and prolong suffering unnecessarily.

Evidence for the degree of such social influences is provided by the conspicuous lack of attention to and, indeed, neglect of the issue of childhood war trauma and lack of treatment facilities in Germany. If there has been a more enlightened trend in recent years, then this is to be welcomed. The number of autobiographical accounts relating to wartime childhood has risen over the last decade. In 1999 there was a small conference devoted to the topic.

The situation in the UK does not appear substantially different, even though the fiftieth anniversary of the Allied victory in 1945 appears to have strengthened the willingness to look beyond the 'tunnel vision' of victorious military exploits and to open our eyes to the darker side of war: the suffering inflicted on children and, amongst them, thousands of evacuee children whose traumatic accounts have been recorded by Wicks (1988). I agree with Wicks when he states in the foreword to his moving book *No Time to Wave Goodbye*:

> For almost 50 years the evacuation of children and mothers from the preconceived danger areas has been pushed into the background, overshadowed by the events of the Second World War that continue to be replayed time and time again. Famous battles, stirring speeches and outstanding heroes have all laid a blanket over a happening that did more to change the face of a nation than a thousand D-Days.
>
> Wicks (1988: X)

I therefore feel tempted to express the view that, throughout history, there has been a collective insensitivity or 'blackout' regarding the impact of war on children in Germany and possibly in Europe as a whole. The sheer number of wars fought on European soil throughout the centuries is astonishing. It appears that wars have been so much a stubborn and accustomed feature of the political landscape on the European continent that for too long they were elevated to the status of legitimate political tools – regardless of the misery of the long-term consequences for children.

The children's crusades of the Middle Ages may represent an aspect of the Dark Ages long since past and swept aside by the so-called progress of civilisation. Yet hardly half a century has passed since children were drafted into the German army during the closing chapter of the Second World War. Dressed up in men's uniforms, these children were forced to fight and to sacrifice their lives.

Fuelled by easily ignitable social forces such as nationalistic and religious fervour, and justified by political paradigms such as war representing the pursuit of politics by other means, wars acquired a notorious tendency of being started and conducted in the name of God.

> He had not the imagination which grasps the meaning of a famine, fire and sword in their effect on individuals, and he resembled the greater number of contemporaries in thinking it more dreadful that the Protestant soldiery should spike out the eyes of an image of the Virgin than that they should hunt the peasants into their burning houses.
>
> Wedgwood ([1938] 1992: 148)

Thus is the Habsburg Emperor Ferdinand II portrayed in C. V. Wedgwood's epic account *The Thirty Years War* which devastated Germany between 1618 and 1648. She portrays the mindset of a politician who wielded enormous power, who never invested much empathy in the 'collateral damage' of civilians, or indeed children, and who, at the end of his life, had 'a tranquil deathbed, propped up among his pillows, fortified by the comforts of the Church, smiling from time to time peacefully at his wife and younger daughter watching by him', and who 'in 18 years of struggle ... had never lost confidence in his mission or in God'; who at the end ... could say "nunc dimittis" with full contentment, for he had indeed achieved a large measure of his ambition' (Wedgwood, [1938] 1992: 409).

If, in her book, C. V. Wedgwood sketched out the prototype of an autocratic leader, then, unfortunately, Emperor Ferdinand II proved to be the rule rather than the exception in European history. In Germany, exercising the levers of power through what Max Weber has defined as 'charismatic domination' (Kershaw, 1991: 10) Hitler catapulted the autocratic tradition of ruling to extremes of despotism and destruction never seen before in Germany. Of course, it is clear that his brand of 'charismatic domination' would never have been successful had there not been centuries of social programming in terms of readiness to accept, rather than challenge, autocratic rules and rulers; to accept subordination rather then free will; to give in to the temptation to follow orders rather than to one's own conscience.

Ample time has been required, and much pain has had to be faced, in order to create the preconditions for a new sensitivity and awareness to emerge which embrace the effects of war on children. To my mind this process has just started. Bearing in mind the long exposure to an autocratic climate, I anticipate that this process will require time, patience and encouragement to succeed.

Individuals tend not to live their lives in isolation from the composition of the wider social consciousness. In clinical terms, this sometimes requires particular attention in order to lift the social 'blinds' shutting out the issue of childhood (post-)war trauma and to initiate a process of creating an awareness and perception of its emotional impact. This may be comparable to an introductory lesson in outlining the issues before the real learning process proceeds.

Sometimes I suggest that books about children and war should be read in order to increase the sensitivity towards the issues involved.

As social traditions and values filter through into families, the families' psychological environment and ambience will influence the development of the children's consciousness. It is easy to see that rigid and autocratic family cultures may be resistant to a more perceptive approach towards children's vulnerabilities by putting up stubborn stumbling blocks that inhibit an enlightened atmosphere where a recognition and respect for the awareness of the childhood (post-)war trauma can flourish.

In a family value system that has been tilted towards glorification of war heroism, admiration for autocratic leadership and the 'strong man' role model and in which the dark side of war has been glossed over and a spider's web of taboos, silence or distortions has been spun, a step-by-step process may be required to defuse the power of such influences, which have been passed down the generations. This may then enable the former (post-)war children to discover the uncensored and untainted reality of their own wartime experiences.

Amongst my clients I have often observed the effect of such obstructive family influences that alienate the children from the real perception of their (post-)war trauma. It seemed as if the children had not been given permission to see with their own eyes and to perceive with their own feelings what they had experienced. Consciously or unconsciously their parents had imposed a dogmatic, if not autocratic, censorship on how or what their children had experienced or how they should have perceived what they had experienced. This, of course, would carry the risk of leaving the children with a false interpretation of reality and thus a sense of detached alienation from their own experience. This is illustrated by the case of Mrs T in 'A Journey into the Abyss of Consciousness. The Story of a Child Witness' in Chapter 3.

'You were such a cheerful child' has been one of the most frequently quoted parental comments recounted by my clients about their (post-)war childhood. As far as the clients were concerned, the assimilation of the parent's misjudgment had to be overcome before they were able to move closer to re-experiencing the drama and trauma of their wartime childhood on their own terms.

'You were so well-behaved and grown-up' is a similar comment that, while demonstrating parental satisfaction over a child's easy handling and behavioural conformity, often reflects a lack of parental sensitivity towards children's true emotional state during the (post-)war years. Being too preoccupied in coping with the circumstances and themselves, the fathers and mothers often proved incapable of sensing and decoding the true emotional state or, indeed, turmoil of their children, or were simply too helpless to face it. Consequently, by misinterpreting their children's maladaptive conformity as an asset rather than as a problem, they neither offered their children support nor consolation, although this would have been required. The lack of emotional support would leave the children lonely and force them into a straitjacket of maladaptive behaviour in order to cope or to survive; at the same time they would have to pay the price of having to sacrifice the expression and fulfilment of their genuine emotional needs.

'You should be glad that you did not suffer the worst things because you were so small' probably ranks as the most shining example of misperceptions because it is based on an image of children being unable to perceive and to be affected by traumatic situations. Without wanting to take a moral stance or to pass judgment, such a view poses a considerable problem, although it may have been expressed with the best of intentions. Firstly, it is based on ignorance about the mental set-up and vulnerability of children. Secondly, the assumption that children were shielded against the perception of trauma due to their age made any supportive intervention appear unneccessary. And thirdly, if such a view was uncritically internalised by the children themselves it may have prevented them from seeking help in order to heal the trauma, thus postponing the treatment of the unresolved trauma for years, if not decades. Therefore the long-term danger of such misperceptions is not just limited to spreading ignorance but lies in discouraging adults to explore, face and heal the real dimension of their war-affected childhood perceptions and mental processes.

Therefore the impact of parental views such as those quoted above may linger on and prevent a solution to the childhood (post-)war trauma. Alienated from an important part of his or her self, because the childhood (post-)war trauma has been barred from consciousness, a former wartime child's sense of self may remain buried under the double weight of early trauma and parental authority – however, ill-founded the latter may be.

Caught between the poles of parentally imposed, dogmatic views and a sense of alienation, the adult may find it difficult to reconnect with his or her true childhood emotions – abandoned like a stranger in his or her own world.

Ignorance and misperceptions may be part of a wider picture of a type of abuse that I define as authoritarian. Installing an appropriate nurturing structure is exchanged for a principle aimed at maintaining parental power at all costs. There is devaluation instead of support, undermining of self-esteem instead of boosting it, criticism instead of encouragement, coldness instead of warmth, harshness and violation of boundaries instead of respect, attacks on a child's individuality and integrity instead of protection, adherence to strict and rigid rules instead of reliance on common sense rules of fair play, pressure to surrender to the will of the parent instead of fostering independence of thought and action, lack of perception of the children's emotional life instead of a finely tuned sensitivity, lack of communication instead of listening and responding in an appropriate way, and there may even be physical attacks, such as beatings instead of solving issues in a non-violent fashion. Instead of trust there is fear, an issue that Franz Kafka (1999) expressed with such excruciating clarity in the opening passage of the famous letter to his father that may well stand as a heartbreaking description and brilliant analysis, but also as an indictment of the authoritarian family system:

> Dearest father,
> You asked me recently why I claim to be frightened of you. As usual, I didn't know how to answer you, partly because I said, I am frightened of you and partly because there are so many components that make up my fear of you that I would not be able to marshal even half of them in conversation. And the very answer I attempt here, in writing, is likely to be incomplete, not only

because my fear of you and its consequences inhibit me, but also because the
enormity of the subject is way above my head and understanding.

Franz Kafka (1999); translated by B. Green

Obviously, if there is an underlying issue of unresolved childhood (post-)war trauma, then the presence of authoritarian abuse associated with low self-esteem, feelings of fear, anxieties and guilt may complicate the situation. The issue of authoritarian abuse may have to be dealt with first, in order to provide a stable platform from which to explore the (post-)war childhood trauma.

Within families, as much as in societies at large, gender role models are influential. Their influence, too, may hinder attempts to reach out towards uncovering long-buried childhood (post-)war trauma.

To my mind, the devaluation, domination or even ruthless suppression of feelings through a code of masculinity based on physical strength, willpower and control make their presence still very much felt. Rather than being welcoming and open towards the flow of feelings to enrich the conduct of their lives, the fists of a macho-like toughness or the reverence of the 'stiff upper lip' approach are being upheld, or even revered, which pushes those men into the desert of alienation from the oasis of emotions.

Acting as a suppressor of emotional complexities, the crippling influence of such a male gender role model may create individuals who are blind and inattentive to emotional needs and sophistication, and to the nurturing of childhood emotions in themselves and others.

The influence of this type of a role model is therefore likely to hamper access to childhood (post-)war traumas. The fear of removing the armoury of this male role model may prevent attempts to deal with the underlying untreated childhood (post-)war trauma and lead to long-term psychological damage.

The invisible threads of family, social, historical and value influences that affect an individual and his or her experiential space beyond the issue of (post-)war trauma in childhood may appear bewildering. However, they should not discourage the professional from patiently untying the knots. Mental health is not about fitting human beings into straitjackets of models but perceiving the complexities of their realities and making them the starting point for explorations

Years ago I came across a booklet of poems written for children during the First World War. Colourful pictures and cheerful rhymes conveyed the impression of war being some kind of glorious party. There was no reference to the apocalypse of war as expressed by eyewitness accounts, such as that of the British war correspondent Philip Gibbs who wrote about the battle of the Somme:

> Victory! ... Some of the German young boys, too young to be killed for old men's crimes, and others might have been old or young. One could not tell because they had no faces, and were just masses of raw flesh in rags of uniforms. Legs and arms lay separate without any bodies thereabouts.
>
> Quoted in Gilbert (1994: 257)

Gibb's voice seemed in vain, as seemed Erich Maria Remarque's famous book *All Quiet on the Western Front* (1929) about the First World War, considering the fact that another, even more devastating war broke out just about two decades after the end of the First World War.

This appears to suggest that the raising awareness of psychological trauma associated with war is a slow and painful process. The length of time it takes for (post-)war trauma in childhood to enter the arena of a wider public consciousness contrasts with the huge number of people engulfed by the flames of war in their childhood and youth.

This may seem strange in the face of enormous advances in other sectors of social development. Yet experience shows that social processes move only at a slow pace when it comes to detaching the collective consciousness from hollow aspirations of illusions of glory and to making it face the senseless sacrifices that had to be made. It appears that a critical approach to war and its horror may not be embraced willingly as long as it is perceived as a threat to the very foundation of a society's concept of civilisation. This may seem odd but not without logic considering as to how much of what has been defined throughout history in erms of progress and achievement appears to be founded on the deeds and deology of war – exemplified by the dictum of the Ancient Greeks, the founders of European civilisation, according to which 'War is the father of all things'.

It may be worth bearing in mind how much time was required, and how many truggles had to be fought, before the reality and consequences of sexual abuse n childhood were recognised and considered to be of sufficient psychological mportance to merit serious professional attention. This may give encouragement o the hope that matters will improve eventually when it comes to dealing with he issue of (post-)war childhood. Yet an independent observer may consider it a paradox that it appears to be easier to set foot on Mars than to look back at the hildhoods on this planet that have been and still remain overshadowed by war.

CHAPTER 6

TO SEE OR NOT TO SEE ... THE UNCONSCIOUS. THE ROLE OF INTUITION

You think that was the end of it? There is a final act to this comedy. Having tried to construct the orbit by using the equation I had just discovered, I made an error in geometry, and failed again. In despair, I threw out the formula, in order to try a new hypothesis, namely that the orbit might be an ellipse. When I had constructed such a figure, by means of geometry, I saw of course that the two methods produced the same result, and that my equation was, in fact, the mathematical expression of an ellipse. Imagine, Doctor, my amazement, joy & embarassment. I had been staring at the solution, without recognizing it! Now I was able to express the thing as law, simple, elegant, and true: The planets move in ellipses with the sun at one focus.

Johannes Kepler, in a letter to D. Fabricius, Easter 1605

There is, indeed, a touch of real mystery [here]. Only we knew [the result in advance], we might be forced, by slow stages, to correct form of Ψ_q. But why was Ramanujan certain there was one? Theoretical insight, to be the explanation, had to be of an order hardly to be credited. Yet it is hard to see what numerical instances could have been available to suggest so strong a result. And unless the form of Ψ_q was known already, no numerical evidence could suggest anything of the kind – there seems no escape, at least, from the conclusion that the discovery of the correct form was a single stroke of insight.

The mathematician J. E. Littlewood on the thinking of
the Indian mathematical genius Srinivasa Ramanujan,
quoted in Kanigel (1992)

To gaze is to think.

Salvador Dali

INTUITION.
THE STRUGGLE TO COMPREHEND

In any scientific field it is important to present observations, conclusion drawn from such observations and to describe the instruments or methods tha enabled the observations to be made, whether by telescope, a biochemical assa or the logical steps of a an abstract mathematical proof.

Having presented conclusions derived from such observations, does raise th question as to the method which I applied in order to discover the childhoo (post-)war trauma. I am, of course, familiar with standard 'instruments' o psychiatric and psychotherapeutic practice such as taking a clinical history formulating an assessment and using deductive thinking. It is evident from th case histories, however, that the discovery of the early (post-)war childhoo rauma was not achieved through the application of the above-mentioned methods. Nor did I obtain the results by following the teachings or principles of particular psychotherapeutic or family therapeutic school. Therefore this raises he question as to how I arrived at the discoveries the way I did and whether my pproach of working constitutes a method.

I will commence by saying that it is probably correct to define my approach s being intuitive in the sense of having been obtained through 'immediate pprehension by the mind without reasoning' *The Concise Oxford Dictionary* 1990). Such a definition seems concordant with the fact that I did not apply any ogical procedure and that I did not adhere to any established psychotherapeutic vay of working while discovering the childhood (post-)war trauma.

Inasmuch as there is little difficulty in terms of defining my approach as ntuitive, the professional acceptance of such an approach was far from secured. n the early 1980s the professional attitude prevailing in Germany, and also in the Jnited Kingdom, was one of perceiving intuition as being very much a second-class method in comparison to the towering dominance of logical reason and he edifice of scientific methods based on logical foundations. Pursuing intuitive iscoveries along the lines I have described in this book and, in addition, being nable to define the operational logistics of intuitive processes, proved too far emoved from the mainstream of the logic-scientific culture. I therefore found nyself working in a quiet corner of more or less benign disregard.

Rather than feeling discouraged by this set of circumstances, it inspired me o pursue and to develop my intuitive style, as I firmly believed that there was certain parallel to what I had experienced in relation to (post-)war childhood rauma.

In my view the whole issue and dimension of (post-)war childhood trauma ad not been seen due to a variety of blinding influences which I have described reviously. Similarly, I felt there was a lack of awareness regarding the fundamental mportance of intuition in general and, specifically, in relation to its potential to ncover unconsciously stored early experiences and trauma, a potential which efied conventional thinking. Of course, there is always the possibility of being roved wrong. However, for a decade, a combination of naivety, curiosity and a lifelong fascination with the observation of processes taking place in my own mind maintained a stubborn belief that insights into the nature of such intuitive processes would emerge eventually.

However, throughout this period, despite there being an abundance of confidence in my belief, there was very little progress to show in terms of advancing my understanding of the intuitive processes. When I was asked to explain how I had arrived at a particular discovery, I was left with little choice but to say that I had not thought about it at all. What I meant was that I had not developed any particular thoughts or weighed any arguments, nor consciously designed any plans or strategies as to how to achieve a particular discovery. Quite simply, the insights which had emerged seemed to have been synthesised outside the radius of conscious thinking.

In the early 1980s I remember sometimes feeling so surprised about the insights that had entered my mind that I wondered whether they could actually have been produced within me or whether they had been 'implanted' into my mind by the action of some magical external force. Slowly, however, I began to accept that the intuitive insights had, in fact, been produced by my own mind. In addition, I gradually came to realise that the quality of intuitive insights was not at all of a haphazard or guesswork-type nature. It became evident to me that their sharpness and reliability in guiding me to core traumatic issues were far superior to any result obtained through the application of logical thinking because a purely logical approach would, in the first instance, not have provided the sense of direction needed to find the trauma. Logical thinking might have enabled me to prove with hindsight how I had arrived at B starting off from A. However, it would not have provided me with the compass to direct me from A to B in the first instance.

Although I became increasingly aware of the superiority, simplicity and elegance of the intuitive approach, I needed time to become accustomed to the operational presence of this unusual force in my mind. This involved unlearning some mental programming, as I had been educated and trained in a variety of areas in which logical thinking was the undisputed 'king'. Never having had the benefit of any formal tuition on the subject of intuition, I needed time for conversion' to take place towards fully embracing the intuitive approach and, in particular, towards developing the notion of there being an operational method at work. Although I had come consciously to realise the immensely fruitful output of the intuitive processes, strangely enough my mindset was still hesitant in accepting the radical idea of my intuitive forces being able to achieve what they did autonomously, without support and guidance from logical thinking. These last remnants of 'old thinking' melted away in the early 1990s, however, when the enlightenment of a new awareness enabled me to see aspects of intuitive processing which, until then, I had failed to see.

Suddenly, I was able to see and to appreciate fully the fascinating capabilities of intuitive processes. I was able to see that the feeling of an 'empty mind' or an 'open mind', to use an expression of the famous Hungarian mathematician Paul Erdös (quoted in Hoffman, 1998: 3, 6), represented more than that of a fancy psychological state. It was the prerequisite for my mind to be able to register perceptions as accurately and as finely tuned as possible without blockage, divertion or derailment by preconceived thoughts or concepts.

Suddenly, I was able to see how important it had been for me to learn to exercise restraint as far as conscious reflections were concerned as they should not interfere with the subtle development of ongoing intuitive hunches. These hunches had to be allowed to run their course and to ripen towards fruition. I realised that allowing conscious thoughts to interfere would only have disrupted, or possibly destroyed, the intricacy of the self-organising dynamics of the intuitive processes taking place.

Suddenly, I realised that it had not been a sign of professional incompetence whenever I happened to be sitting in my chair unable to utter a word about what was intending to do. As I was able to see now, intuitive processes required a gestation period before their final products — namely ideas — had crystallised sufficiently in my mind in order to be assigned the labels of verbal terminology.

Suddenly, I was able to comprehend that it was not due to magic when I had the sensation of my hands appearing to be guided by their own impulses. What happened was that they simply followed intuitive 'instructions' that were too subtle and sophisticated to be registered or even initiated by rational planning.

Suddenly, I became aware of the whole picture of the innovative flair of th intuitive forces, not unlike the famous astronomer Johannes Kepler who state that he had 'been staring at the solution without recognising it'. The solutio was that the intuitive processes evolved in a self-organised style made distinc by its high efficiency and, at the same time, elegance. It was the sheer flair an magic of the inherent dynamics which propelled them towards the constructio of insights, be it images, object sculpts or even verbal interpretations. The poetic flowing quality whose comprehension had eluded me for so long, reflecte the very essence of these dynamics. There was no sharp distinction betwee perception and thinking. Whatever images or communicative patterns I ha perceived through the assistance of my sensory organs, they were absorbed an assimilated in order to catalyse their transformation into insights. Thus, ther was a flow-like continuum, starting with perception and leading towards insight which represented the 'conveyor belt' that produced images, designs of objec configurations and thoughts.

The 'empty mind', or the state of 'zero knowledge', was the point o departure. Subtle hunches which were much too fine to be expressed in words the sensation of 'knowing without knowing', the subthreshold awareness of th design of object sculpts even in the absence of a rational definable plan; the all represented intermediate stages in this fascinating evolution of convertin 'zero knowledge' into insights. At the end there was the miraculous ability to fin words for what had been created intuitively, culminating in knowledge wher there had been none before.

Breaking through the shell of the unconscious, self-organising intuitiv processes were not random occurences; rather, they were crucial providers o insights into understanding issues where there had been no previous consciou understanding. By not interfering with intuitive dynamics, and by allowing menta processes to take their natural course in order to design their own solution, I ha been able to pick the fruits of their activities.

It had become clear to me that the crucial aspect of my method had been tha I had not adhered to any particular method. For many years, this had proved distinct disadvantage, but the logic of this decision had now become apparent.

Had I tried to impose a pre-existing psychotherapeutic method on my way of intuitive thinking I would have stopped its heartbeart, because the intuitive method relied on its own immanent method of synthesising knowledge about early experiences and trauma drawn from patterns of communication. Therefore there was no need to superimpose a method, because the intuitive dynamics followed their own method. All I had to do was to grant the intuitive method its own space, time and freedom to evolve according to its own laws of operation.

The paradox had been solved: an intuitive approach which appeared to have lacked the ingredients of any established method had turned out to be grounded in its own operating method.

PERCEPTUAL THINKING.
THE CAPACITY OF LOOKING INTO THE EARLY WORLD OF TRAUMA

It is evident from the case histories presented that the discovery of early experiences was made possible by an approach of relying on intuition. While attempting to obtain a clearer understanding of the role of intuitive perception and intuitive thinking in the production of intuitive insights I had to rely on observing the processes unfolding in my mind. However much it may be possible to differentiate between perception and thinking, my observations suggested that it was difficult to make such a clear distinction. I was able to perceive certain impressions such as facial expressions, sounds of voice or patterns of body movements, even if their subtlety would often make it difficult for me to define such impressions with precision.

Usually, however, such perceptions did not represent an experience that could have been defined as an isolated phenomenon. Instead, I experienced a self-organised, evolutionary process that would transform the perception of an impression into an internal image and then into an insight, as if there was an automatic production line designed towards generating insights from perceptions. Therefore, the lack of a clear distinction between perception and thinking suggested to me the intimately interlinked nature of both intuitive perception and intuitive thinking within the context of intuitive processing. I order to emphasise this aspect of a confluent interlinkage regarding intuitiv perception and intuitive thinking, I am suggesting the term 'perceptual thinking while stressing once more that this is a view drawing on the observation c intuitive processes as they evolve within my mind.

The case histories illustrate the intuitive approach's capacity to pinpoint an discover such early experiences or trauma surprisingly accurately, swiftly an reliably, even where there has been a lack of verbal information and consciou access. Last but not least, the intuitive production of the insights occurre outside the influence of logical manoeuvring, although the 'end product' c the intuitive processing – namely, the insights – was, of course, open to logica consideration and scrutiny.

The accurate perception of early experiences and trauma has alway especially intrigued me. I never cease to be amazed by the brilliant ability of th human sensory and thought processing system to convert information that i transmitted by 'bytes' of visual, auditory data or other sensory modalities int insights. I cannot help but to express my profound admiration for what I conside the sheer wonder of human communication, whose heights of sophistication are at least to my mind, still far from being fully explored.

Examining the findings from the case illustrations more closely, it is possibl to deduce several operational features of the workings of intuitive perceptio and thinking, i.e. perceptual thinking. Firstly, many of the case histories in thi book, and those described in previous publications (in particular in Heinl, 1987c 1988, 1991, 1994a, 1998, 2000), illustrate the capacity of perceptual thinkin to 'pick up' infant life experiences. The image of the hungry baby in 'A spell c Dizziness' and that of the little girl who feels cold in the 'Mysterious Depressior in Chapter 1 not only point at particular events – namely, hunger due to starvatio and exposure to cold – but also at the time at which these experiences too place. The degree of accuracy that can be achieved by perceptual thinking i further illustrated by the following story.

On one occasion, when entering the seminar room after a break, I saw on of the seminar participants, a woman, lying relaxed on the floor. The way she la down and had her face turned towards the sun and the way her eyes blinked in the sunshine, reminded me instantly of a little baby lying in its cot on a terrace covered by a glass roof and enjoying exposure to the sunlight. So strong was the confidence of my perception that I told the woman that this was what she must have been experiencing, when she was a baby.

The woman was courteous enough to listen to my spontaneous hypothesis before replying that it could not be true. However, even more to the point was the argument she used in order to refute what I had postulated. Although she had been born in early springtime, and although the affluent parental home had, indeed, had a large terrace covered by a glass roof, she could not possibly have enjoyed the sunshine on the terrace because, as she said, the parental home had been bombed to the ground immediately after her birth.

This swift and elegant rebuttal would seem to have signalled the end of my lofty hypothesis, had I not asked the woman to be kind enough to check the exact date of the destruction of the house through an independent source. She agreed to contact her mother, who confirmed that she had, indeed, placed her infant daughter's little cot on the terrace so that she could enjoy the sunshine. Her mother clearly remembered having done so for several months, as the house with its terrace was only bombed a few months *after* her daughter's birth. I like to add that such accurate perception of the age at which a given experience or trauma occurred is by no means the exception.

Secondly, apart from being capable of 'scanning' adult behavioural and communicative patterns for early experiences and determining the age at which they occurred, intuitive perception and intuitive thinking, i.e. perceptual thinking, appear successful in extracting information about the quality of early relationships. Again, the case histories, such as 'The Enigma of the Desert' or 'The Silver Necklace' in Chapter 3, provide evidence for the capacity of perceptual thinking to uncover the emotional flavour of early relationships. These case stories, as well as the story described in 'Object Sculpting, Symbolic Communication and Early Experience: A Single Case Study' (Heinl, 1988) underline the fact that the quality of such early relationships was established without prior verbal exploration.

155

I like to illustrate this capacity by turning to the following story of a woman who had asked me to assist her in exploring the relationship to her father who had succumbed to war injuries as a young adult. The woman told me that her psychotherapist had expressed the view that she was suffering from a 'fixation' on her father. When I listened to the woman's account my intuitive perception made me feel unable to agree with the psychotherapist's assessment. I therefore told the woman that I saw no indication of a 'fixation'. In fact, my intuitive perception of the daughter-father relationship suggested to me that the early relationship between her and her father had been a warm and cordial one.

Hearing my perception of the relationship, the woman reacted with a sense of relief. Then, when she showed me photographs of her father, I saw the picture of a man with soft and sad eyes who radiated a warm atmosphere around him as if to touch the onlooker with his gentleness. Thus, having obtained more tangible evidence for my view, I emphasised once more that I failed to see a particular problem in having had such a loving father. The woman's eyes filled with tears because my view concurred exactly with what she had felt throughout her life without ever having dared to express it openly.

The example of the woman cited above shows the value of the accurate detection of the quality of this early relationship, particularly in the context of (post-)war trauma in childhood. It shows how helpful it was for the woman to obtain a conscious awareness of her very positive relationship to her father as this strengthened her belief in her own perception. It allowed her openly to accept the positive relationship to her father and facilitated the mourning of his early loss. Particularly in those cases where the early landscape of war experience has been overshadowed by losses, the conscious awareness of a positive early relationship can provide a much needed candle of warmth and light in a landscape of darkness.

Thirdly, there is evidence to suggest that perceptual thinking is capable of discovering the emotional flavour of whole networks of early relationships. 'The Silver Necklace' in Chapter 3 provides a striking example for this capacity, as does the above mentioned publication (Heinl, 1988) in which the emotional flair of a network of carers in hospital was established accurately.

Although the mental logistics and algorithms through which these insights are achieved are still unclear, it is evident that perceptual thinking possesses an astounding ability in terms of distilling crucial and, indeed, interconnected aspects of early experiences from patterns of adult communication. Looking at points one to three together it is tempting to argue that perceptual thinking is intrinsically capable of discovering and processing developmentally relevant information which is transmitted by a given individual. The 'radar screen' of intuitive perception appears capable of not only spotting aspects which are relevant to an adult's mental state and frame of mind at the present, but also aspects which are connected to his or her infancy, such as experiences or trauma, infant-parent relationships and the systemic network of the surrounding field of the family or carers.

I cannot help reiterating my admiration and, indeed, sense of wonder for intuitive perception and intuitive thinking, i.e. perceptual thinking, – tools that analyse and synthesise received communicative 'bytes' of sensory 'data' to such an effect. In daily life, one may easily forget the extent to which the astonishing workings of the mind, involving the construction of insights based on perceptions, are based on the finely tuned and highly complex mental 'machinery'.

However, Sacks's book *The Man Who Mistook His Wife for a Hat* (1985) and Ramachandran and Blakeslee's *Phantoms in the Brain* (1998) provide dramatic evidence for the degree to which mental activity, including communication, depends on proper neuronal processing. Bauby's extraordinary account *The Diving-Bell and the Butterfly* (1997) demonstrates the bewildering extent to which the ability to communicate may be destroyed, despite the preservation of the potential for communication.

If perceptual thinking is capable of discovering early experiences and, indeed, networks of such experiences, then it appears plausible to assume that such information has to be contained in the patterns of communication transmitted by the various adults, even if such information has not been articulated verbally. To put it in a slightly different way: if I was the recipient of 'waves' of communication, what, if any, deductions can be drawn about the nature of the communication conveyed to me by the various adults concerned? This turns the focus of attention away from the processes taking place in my mind and toward the source of information transmitted to me through communication.

If the capacity of perceptual thinking is such as to be able to scan and screen adult behavioural and communicative patterns for early experiences, then it has to be assumed that the source of such patterns lies within the individuals who communicate them to me. The man in 'A Spell of Dizziness' or the woman in 'The Mysterious Depression' in Chapter 1 must have sent out communicative signals which contained information about their early lives. Quite clearly, if that had not been the case, I would not have been able to perceive such information. But how could anyone transmit information about his or her early life without doing so consciously?

Evidently human communication represents an extremely complex system or, indeed, network of interconnected organs whose successful function depends on the seamless interaction of brain, nerve and muscular activities involving various organs. At the same time, the communicative system of any given individual has to be considered as a biological system with a developmental background. Its uniquely personal features have developed over time in terms of their dynamics of control, interplay of various components, sound profile and, indeed, responsiveness during verbal or non-verbal interactions.

Therefore the development of a child's communicative system, in terms of 'output' features such as vocal or facial expression or gestures or 'input' features such as listening, appears to be influenced and shaped by the impact of positive and negative interactional and educational forces. Taking this into account I have developed the concept of the 'communicative body' (Heinl, 1991). It is based on the idea that such forces, be they positive or negative experiences or trauma, are likely to affect the operation of the communicative system in such a way as to leave clearly perceptible or coded 'footprints', which will then be 'interwoven' into the patterns of communication.

Sometimes such 'footprints' may be fairly easily noticed, but there are occasions where their perception proves much more difficult because the impact of the early experiences has been coded. Nevertheless, even in the latter case, evidence suggests that the 'antennae' of intuitive perception appear to be equipped with a 'decoder' sufficiently sensitive to be able to 'pick up' the traumatic experiences amidst the flow of adult communication.

If the concept of the 'communicative body' is meaningful, it would attribute a dual role to adult communication. Firstly, adult communication would fulfil the function of distribution of any content, such as talking, about any possible topic. Such distribution of content would be unrelated to a given individual's background, unless, of course, there was an exchange of information about aspects of the background that are consciously accessible.

Secondly, the adult communication would represent the vehicle that conveys more or less coded messages about a given individual's early background. The important point here is that such a transmission of coded information would occur all the time because it is an inbuilt feature of the development of a given individual's 'communicative body'. Furthermore, this would occur even in the absence of the adults' conscious awareness, because the early experiences or trauma in question may have remained unconscious as they have been built into the design of the 'communicative body'. The transmission of early experiences through the 'communicative body' would, of course, include the transmission of traumatic experiences. Case reports such as 'A Spell of Dizziness' in Chapter 1 suggest that this may produce symptoms whose subtle and coded presentation may not be easily recognisable, unlike classical symptoms such as depression or anxiety that are based on phenomenological criteria rather than taking into account the impact of early traumatic experiences on communicative patterns (Heinl, 1994).

In order to illustrate the duality, I like to refer to the sound profile of a Stradivarius violin. Such a violin may distribute musical content in terms of sounds by any composer's music. Simultaneously, the violin will transmit a uniquely individual sound profile that is due to its 'communicative body', and that in turn is a result of this particular violin's developmental history of having been manufactured by Stradivari.

The sound profile of a particular Stradivarius violin may not be recognised by most people, including myself! However, I understand that the characteristics of a particular violin can be recognised and therefore decoded correctly by an expert. The interplay of the violin's 'communicative body' with the sharpness of the expert's auditory, and possibly intuitive, perception would allow the correct identification of the violin in question. Similarly, the combination of a individual's 'communicative body' and of the intuitive perception and intuitive thinking of an appropriate expert would allow the possibility of looking into the early space of experience.

There is no doubt as to the enormous importance of John Bowlby's (197? pioneering concept of attachment theory for infant development which has provided an understanding of the central role of attachment of children to their mothers, and indeed fathers, for the development of their personality.

Based on John Bowlby's work Mary Main and her colleagues (1985) have described several types of attachment patterns of children to their mothers patterns that are already discernible in early childhood and that show stability over time. Mary Main and her co-workers have therefore developed the notion of a link between children's and adults' behaviour in terms of the maintenance of attachment patterns.

Bearing in mind the stability of different types of attachment patterns over time, I am inclined to speculate that attachment patterns may be perceived a an intuitive level in adults. I would like to stress that I do not want to go as far as claiming that the quality of relationships brought to light in such exploration equals specific types of attachment patterns in terms of their research definition However, I do feel that perceptual thinking enabled me to pinpoint important aspects of early relationships accurately, including the wider framework of early networks of relationships.

What has emerged is the capacity of perceptual thinking to access early experiences and to highlight aspects of adult human communication that reflect this early developmental background. Trees may be huge and 'adult', but a cross section quickly reveals very important clues about their early development Communication, by carrying information about early life, provides a powerful linkage between the infant's and adult's spaces of experience. Likewise intuitive perception and intuitive thinking appear to provide the 'instrument' for the successful discovery of this linkage.

If my perceptual thinking appears to have such a capacity in terms of screening current patterns of adult communication for evidence of past experiences, then, at the same time, I do not wish to ascribe myself paranormal abilities; rather, I feel that the ability to recognise features of past behaviours in humans reflects, basically, a human capacity. If the famous painter Max Ernst once stated that every human being is a painter, I am inclined to believe that there is the intrinsic capacity in every human being of spotting behavioural features in other human beings which appear to be rooted in the past – even if this is limited to conclusions such as a particular adult behaving 'like a baby'.

It is difficult to say what is more astounding: the extent to which perceptual thinking is capable of identifying features of past age in relation to current age and the extent to which such perceptual data are being transformed into coherent insights, or the extent to which such processing occurs quasi-automatically – namely, in a self-organised style.

Of course, this raises intriguing and fundamental questions about the working of, as Johannes Kepler put it in 1610, 'the mysterious firmament contained within the skull'. What kind of sensory perception, what kind of neuronal networking logistics, what kind of mental algorithms are involved in the astonishing achievement of insight creation? What neuronal hardware, software, chips, fibres, amplifiers, filters, for instance, guided the perception of a virtual stranger – Dr A in 'The Silver Necklace' in Chapter 3 – to be transformed into an object sculpt that turned out to be meaningful to his early life story?

These are fascinating questions, as they touch on the heart of initiatives aimed at unravelling how the mind processes perceptions, makes connections and produces new meaningful insights. This is undoubtedly a fascinating field, and the wealth of open questions suggests that at the start of a new millennium they do not signal the beginning of the end in psychological science, but rather the end of the beginning.

OBJECT SCULPTS.
LEVELS OF MEANING AND SPACE-TIME
TRANSFORMATIONS

To have many objects present in the mind and, with a light touch, to bring the most distant ones to relate to each other ...

Johann Wolfgang von Goethes's definition of genius,
quoted in Musil (1952); my translation

From now on, space and time separately have vanished into the merest shadows, and only a sort of combination of the two preserves any reality.

Herrmann Minkowski, German mathematician, 1907,
quoted in Brian (1996)

The normal adult does not reflect about problems of space and time. In his view, everything there is to think about these problems he has already accomplished in infancy. However, my development has been so slow that I only started to wonder at space and time when I was already an adult. Naturally I then penetrated deeper into the problems than an ordinary child.

Albert Einstein, quoted in Wickert (1972); my translation

The way in which the design of an object sculpt forms in my mind has never ceased to intrigue me. Each object sculpt is unique in its composition of objects, colours and design. Each displayed its individual spatial composition and conveyed its unique atmosphere through patterns of wordless communication

Extremely sensitive to even subtle changes of position, mutual distances or choice of the objects involved, the object sculpts demonstrated a wealth and variety of expression, consistent with the systemic principle that the information contained in such a network of objects is always greater than that of the sum of its parts.

I was even more intrigued to observe, over and over again, that the object sculpts proved to be relevant and meaningful to those individuals for whom I had constructed them. How could an assembly of little objects of simple design possibly produce such powerful effects on individuals in the sense of rendering unconscious experiences conscious?

Taken at face value, an object sculpt consists of three-dimensional objects of different geometrical sizes, shapes and colours. Strictly speaking, such objects embody visual phenomena that carry no meaning. It is only through the use of verbal language and the labelling through verbal descriptions that they acquire meaning. Therefore the attachment of the description 'orange cube' to an object with such features will elevate this particular object from a non-lingual, visual level to a level of meaning once the object has been assigned the meaning 'orange cube'. An orange cube can then be perceived as a representative of a distinct class of phenomena; that is, it is different from a red cube, a violet circle or a pink flower, for instance.

The accounts of the various object sculpts suggest that the individuals concerned did more than simply perceive the objects displayed in front of them. Looking more closely at their responses shows that they did more than just absorb the visual experience of the objects laid out in front of them and more than just attach verbal definitions to the individual objects, and, indeed, to the whole design of the object sculpt.

It appears that mental operations took place which were aimed at injecting sets of meaning in the individual objects and the object sculpt as a whole. These sets of meanings transcended the verbal definitions of the objects. Frequently, for instance, the little pink koala bear was identified as representing a small child, a baby or the individual himself or herself in childhood or infancy. Likewise the lion and the rabbit were perceived to reflect parental figures where usually, but not always, the lion would stand for the father. Similarly, other objects wer assigned meanings that went beyond the level of simple object descriptions.

At times, such injections of personal meaning involved assigning to an objec object a symbolic meaning, such as conceptualising a black box as a symbol of grave. Typically such injections of personal meaning involved the experience c emotions triggered by the perception of the object sculpt, such as in 'A Journe in the Abyss of Consciousness. The Story of a Child Witness' in Chapter 3 Usually, another intriguing feature emerged – namely, a subtle shift of the tim framework of reference. This appeared to be based on subtle transformations c time and space.

In 'The Silver Necklace' in Chapter 3, for instance, Dr A identified the sma koala bear as representing himself in childhood. This may have been an obviou step to take. However, under the circumstances, this step implicitly changed th time framework of the object sculpt. What had been put together in the preser as a collection of objects suddenly underwent a transformation through Dr A interpretation of the object sculpt representing a past mental experience tha had happened in childhood. Obviously such a transformation would not hav been successful without the introduction of the dimension of time.

It may have been a spatial feature of the little koala bear – namely, its sma size, and possibly its small size compared to the larger sizes of other dolls – tha provided the trigger for the introduction of the dimension of time by equallin small size with infancy, i.e. events which happened in the past. The object sculp in 'The Enigma of the Desert' in Chapter 3 makes the transformation of a spatia order into a time framework even more transparent. Indeed, without the menta operation of time transformation the spatial arrangement of the object sculp would have failed to acquire its particular meaning of representing the first yea of life, which parallels the finding of a previous paper (Heinl, 1988).

None of these transformations of meaning took place at my instigation c through rational reflection on the part of the individuals concerned. Dr A account in 'The Silver Necklace' is as typical as Mrs R's account in 'The Enigm of the Desert' in illustrating that the mental operations triggered by the sigh of the object sculpts occurred in an entirely self-organised manner. Wherea itially, the object sculpts may have appeared to represent little more than urious collections of objects assembled at random, closer scrutiny reveals heir remarkable capacity to catalyse sequential levels of meanings towards onstructing complex networks of representations of early experiences. This ppears to be due to object sculpts triggering the transformation of the visual erception of objects into higher levels of thinking capable of generating new evels of meaning; that is, insights in relation to early experiences. The fact that he mental operations occurred in a manner which was self-organising and which id not resort to rational thinking suggests the involvement of the player which I ave described in the previous chapters: intuition.

These considerations facilitate the understanding of the surprising effect f object sculpts on unconsciously stored early traumatic experiences. Let us ssume that the visual object patterns provided by the object sculpt are such hat they evoke similarities to memories which have been stored unconsciously nd which have never been processed consciously. Then the perception of such n object sculpt may set in motion and catalyse mental operations that appear apable of injecting meaning into the hitherto unconscious experiences and thus atapult them into consciousness.

The key effect of object sculpts would therefore consist of catalysing mental perations that transform unconscious experiences into a conscious awareness y facilitating new levels of meaning. Transforming unconscious into conscious naterial, however, does imply that new understanding has been created. herefore the effect of object sculpts would consist of catalysing understanding where there has been no understanding before.

However 'childish' the objects that I have used in the course of my work may ave appeared at first sight, their real importance as catalysts of understanding s hard to overestimate.

INTUITION.
THE ICON OF A NEW THINKING
ABOUT THINKING

It is by logic we prove, it is by intuition we discover.

Henri Poincaré, French mathematician, quoted in Claxton (1997)

While bearing in mind the innovative insights and wealth of understanding that the psychological revolution of the last hundred years has swept into the arena of public knowledge, the issue of psychological trauma, and of war trauma in childhood in particular, provides a salutary reminder as to how long it has taken history to open its eyes and develop sympathetic concern to these dimensions of human suffering.

In a similar manner, and again pointing at the 'selective blindness' of history, the topic of intuition has been condemned to a shadowy existence in cultural European history without there having been a fair appreciation of its enormous and fascinating potential.

Summarising this historical failure due to a cultural mindset dominated by the reductionist sceptre of logic, Claxton (2000) states:

> The distrust of intuition and the inability to see how (and even perhaps, why)
> it could be incorporated into education, reflect 300 years of European cultural
> history. The Cartesian slogan *Cogito ergo sum* encapsulated the successful
> attempt to reduce the human mind only to its most conscious and rational
> regions, and to persuade people that their fundamental identity resided in
> the exercise of this explicit, articulate, analytical form of intelligence. The
> Enlightenment of the eighteenth century picked out just this single way of
> knowing and, in raising it to a high art, implicitly ignored or disabled any

others: those that were not so clinical and cognitive, and were instead more bodily, sensory, affective, mythic or aesthetic – in a word, intuitive.

Claxton (2000: 32)

The dominance of this mindset is surprising, if not paradoxical, bearing in mind the crucial role intuition has played in those very fields that throughout history have been considered as the domains of the true kings of logic – in particular science and mathematics. Dating back to the cradle of science and mathematics in Ancient Greece, over and over again, intuition has shown its mettle and inspirational power in the process of discoveries of new insights within these fields.

While science and mathematics acquired their reputation for representing elegant towers of pure and stringent logic, intuition provided the foundations for these towers to be built on, without the intuition's invaluable groundbreaking work being properly appreciated and recognised in the halls of fame of European cultural history:

> There are examples such as Archimedes finding the principle of displacement in the bath, Kekulé discovering the molecular conformation of benzene thanks to seeing a snake-like structure in his dream, and Poincaré's realization – in the very act of stepping on a bus – that his 'Fuchsian functions' were identical to those of non-Euclidian geometry.
>
> Shepard (1978), quoted in Marton et al. (1994: 458)

Yet history appeared to be one-sided in its applause for logic and in its lack of regard for the crucial role played by intuition in the discovery of new insights.

The famous Indian mathematician Srinivasa Ramanujan (1887–1920) stands out as an intriguing example challenging this one-sided mindset. To this day, Ramanujan has left mathematicians perplexed as to the manner by which he discovered his new insights that he wrote down in his famous notebooks.

Baffled by the enigma of Ramanujan's intuitive power, mathematicians have repeatedly expressed 'wonder and awe in the face of his powers, have stumbled about, groping for words, in trying to convey [his] mystery' (Kanigel, 1992 while Ramanujan himself attributed his insights to divine intervention as h saw 'scrolls containing the most complicated mathematics' unfolding 'before h eyes ... after seeing in dreams the drops of blood that, according to traditio heralded the presence of the god Narasimha, the male consort of the goddes Namagiri' (Kanigel, 1992: 281).

Whereas the mathematician Askey came to the conclusion that 'the enigm of Ramanujan's creative process is still covered by a curtain that has barely bee drawn' (quoted in Kanigel, 1992: 280), the English mathematician Littlewoo a contemporary of Ramanujan, pointed at the very core of the relationsh between logic and intuition by describing Ramanujan as a man for whom

> the clear-cut idea of what is *meant* by proof ... he perhaps did not possess at all; once he had become satisfied of a theorem's truth, he had scant interest in proving it to others. The word *proof*, here, applies in a mathematical sense. And yet, construed more loosely, Ramanujan truly had *nothing to prove*.
>
> Quoted in Kanigel (1992: 358–359)

The puzzling questions raised by Srinivasa Ramanujan's intuitive flair are a poignant as ever and are likely to challenge the dominance of logic in Europea thinking, as its glamour is too much based on the result rather than the intuitiv process that inspired and empowered the minds of the mathematicians an scientists to attain new insights.

Describing the discovery of the proof for Fermat's last theorem Singh (1997 recounts the thrilling climax of an intuitive insight that enabled the Englis mathematician Andrew Wiles to establish the proof.

'Suddenly, totally unexpectedly, I had this incredible revelation', remember Wiles:

> It was a moment of inspiration that Wiles will never forget. As he recounted these moments, the memory was so powerful that he was moved to tears: 'It was so indescribably beautiful; it was so simple and elegant. I couldn't

understand how I'd missed it and I just stared at it in disbelief for twenty minutes. Then during the day I walked around the department, and I'd keep coming back to my desk looking to see if it was still there. It was still there. I couldn't contain myself, I was so excited. It was the most important moment of my working life. Nothing I ever do again will mean as much.'

Singh (1997: 297–298)

Although individual psychotherapists such as Rogers or Beck espoused intuition-friendly views (Bohart, 1999), the field of psychotherapy as a whole appears to have shared the same lack of awareness and disinterest towards the hidden potential of intuition that has affected European cultural history. Intriguingly, however, there have been mathematicians and scientists who have been astutely aware and have reflected on the creative role of intuition during the development of insights.

Poincaré's brilliantly concise statement, quoted above, is as much testimony to such an awareness as Littlewood's reflection on Ramanujan. Hadamard (1949), the French mathematician, was also acutely aware of the vital role of intuition and paid tribute to its unquestionable contribution, when he wrote:

Unconscious activity often plays a decisive part in discovery; that periods of ineffective efforts are often followed, after intervals of rest or distraction, by moments of sudden illumination; that these flashes of inspiration are explicable only as the result of activities of which the agent has been unaware – the evidence for all this seems overwhelming.

Quoted in Kanigel (1992: 285)

More recently, a survey by Marton *et al.* (1994) of winners of the Nobel prize in science, i.e. in physics, chemistry and medicine between 1970–89, provides fascinating reading as it highlights the key role attested to intuition by the laureates themselves.

Seventy-two of the participants in the survey, all eminent scientists, acknowledged scientific intuition. Interestingly, 'the 11 participants who either

denied the existence of scientific intuition or expressed doubts about its natur
actually referred to experiences of the same kind as the other 72 participant:
who recognised scientific intuition', concluded Marton *et al.* (1994). Therefor
there is a virtually universal acknowledgment amongst the Nobel laureates of th
central role of scientific intuition.

By reflecting on the nature of intuition the 1973 laureate in medicine, Konra
Lorenz, concludes:

> This apparatus ... which intuits has to have an enormous basis of known facts
> at its disposal with which to play. And it plays in a very mysterious manner,
> because ... it sort of keeps all known facts afloat, waiting for them to fall
> into place, like a jigsaw puzzle. And if you press ... if you try to permutate
> your knowledge, nothing comes out of it. You must give a sort of mysterious
> pressure, and then rest, and suddenly BING ... the solution comes.
>
> Quoted in Marton *et al.* (1994: 467)

Another Nobel laureate for medicine (1986), Rita Levi-Montalcini, emphasise
the key role of intuition when she states:

> Intuition ... is something subconscious, which, all of a sudden, comes out of a
> clear sky to you and is absolutely a necessity, more than a logic, in any sense
> there is to make a work of art — in art or in science.
>
> Quoted in Marton *et al.* (1994: 463)

Summarising the findings of the survey, Marton *et al.* (1994) state that

> Scientific intuition is seen as an alternative to normal step-by-step logical
> reasoning. The scientists do something or something happens to them
> without them being aware of the reasons of the antecedents. The acts of the
> events are, however, guided or accompanied by feelings which sometimes
> spring form a quasi-sensory experience. Intuition is closely associated with
> a sense of direction, it is more often about finding a path than arriving at

an answer or reaching a goal. The ascent of intuition is rooted in extended, varied experience of the object research: although it may feel as if it comes out of the blue, it does not come out of the blue. The most fundamental aspect of scientific intuition is that the scientists choose directions or find solutions for which they do not have sufficient data in the computational sense. The explanation must thus point to a process which is an alternative to a logical calculus.

Marton *et al.* (1994: 468)

Fortunately, the survey by Marton *et al.* (1994) appears to exemplify more of a trend than an isolated preoccupation with the issue of intuition, as more recent times have seen a sea change in attitude towards intuition. Researchers are turning their eyes towards trying to unravel the mysteries of the mental processes and operations underlying intuition. 'This fascinating research ... offers a profound and salutary challenge to our everyday view of our own minds and how they work,' argues Claxton (1997: 4). While emphasising that 'These empirical demonstrations are more than interesting: they are important,' Claxton refers to the observation that 'our ideas, and often our best, most ingenious ideas, do not arrive as the result of faultless chains of reasoning. They "occur to us". They "pop into our heads". They came out of the blue' (1997: 49).

Applying a more systematic description, Claxton differentiates seven 'facets of intuition' that help to illuminate and clarify the phenomenon of intuition. First, there appears to be an agreement 'that intuition is a *different way* of knowing, one which does not rely on articulate fluency' and that is 'the opposition ... to thinking that is abstract, logical or analytical'. Second, intuition possesses a quality of providing a 'sense of the relationships between the various elements of a situation or a problem. By contrast with analytical thinking, intuition is thought of as synthetic, giving a sense of the structure of the whole, which may well be greater than the sum of its parts'. Third, 'there is a view that intuition involves reframing or reconceptualising the situation', which 'typically involves reorganisation of the perception of the problem, often as a result of breaking through an unconscious assumption which had been effectively blocking a

171

situation'. Fourth, there appears a linkage between intuition and experience in the sense of 'often ... drawing upon and extracting meaning from a largely tacit database of first-hand experience', rather than from 'rational deduction'. Fifth, intuition appears to be associated with an 'essentially affective tone, an emotional involvement on the part of the owner'. Sixth, there is 'the familiar assumption that intuition relies upon mental processes that are not conscious operations which may actually be impeded by the effort to make them conscious or to bring them under conscious control'. Seventh, 'intuition comes with a kind of built-in confidence rating, a subjective feeling of "rightness", that may vary in its strength from "complete guess" to "absolute certainty"' (Claxton, 2000: 32).

The results of the research are also highlighting mental attitudes or the kind of beneficial internal mental environment so to speak, that constitute prerequisite for the intuitive potential to develop and flourish. As intuitive insights require time, i.e. a gestation period, the virtue of patience is required. 'The importance of "daring to wait" can hardly be overstated' (Claxton, 2000: 49). 'You keep asking this question continually, over years, ... it's a lifetime,' states Lipscomb, the 1973 Nobel prize winner for chemistry, thus emphasising the need for patience (quoted in Marton et al., 1994: 465).

'[Y]ou have been thinking about something without willing to for a long time ... Then, all of a sudden, the problem is opened to you in a flash, and you suddenly see the answer,' states Rita Levi-Montalcini, the Nobel laureate for medicine in 1986 (quoted in Marton et al., 1984: 462). Her account provides another example for the patience required to wait for an eventual insight.

In contrast, however,

> pressure and stress of any kind ... are anathema to intuition, as they tend to focus perception and cognition on a predetermined range of strategies and information — to those that are 'obvious' or 'normal' — and thus to remove the breadth and open-mindedness of visions which may be required to uncover a false assumption or a creative analogy.
>
> Easterbrook (1959)

A mental attitude of being able to 'explore uncertainties and to entertain doubts' and to 'live with these doubts and uncertainties without fear' – traits which have been shown to be typical for 'successful intuitives' (Claxton, 1997: 73–74, citing research by Westcott, 1968) – is important, as well as the capacity to maintain a sense of confidence. This is illustrated by the example of Max Planck, when he stated:

> My vain attempts to somehow reconcile the elementary quantum with classical theory continued for many years and cost me great effort. Many of my colleagues saw almost a tragedy in this, but I saw it differently because the profound clarification of my thoughts I derived from this work had great value for me.
>
> Quoted in Segrè (1980: 76)

A mental attitude of openness and willingness to surrender and trust what might be seen as a sense of direction, or even 'supernatural' guidance, is also vital.

> And so ... as we did our work, I think, we almost felt at times that there was almost a hand guiding us. Because we would go from one step to the next, and somehow we would know which was the right way to go. And I really can't tell how we knew that, how we knew that it was necessary to move ahead,

reflects the 1985 Nobel prize winner for medicine Michael Brown on his experience (quoted in Marton et al., 1994: 461–462).

However much there may be boundaries between logic and art in the real world, intuitive processes are not affected by such restraints, as it is evident from the comment of Paul Berg, the 1980 Nobel prize winner for chemistry, when he says:

> There is another aspect that I would add to it, and that is, I think, taste. Taste in almost the artistic sense. Certain individuals see art in some undefinable way, can put together something which has a certain style, or a certain class to it. A certain rightness to it.
>
> Quoted in Marton *et al.* (1994: 463)

Emphasising the sheer sensual quality of his intuitive thinking, Alber Einstein, a firm advocate of intuition, came to the conclusion that God had no only given him 'the stubbornness of a mule' but also 'a keen sense of smel (quoted in Segrè, 1980: 100).

As an ever-curious and perceptive observer of his intuitive processes, Alber Einstein noted that his insights often preceded language: 'These thoughts di not come in any verbal formulation. I very rarely think in words at all. A though comes, and I may try to express it in words afterwards' (quoted in Schooler *et al* 1993: 166). Studying the relationship between insight creation and verbalisatio further, Schooler *et al.* (1993: 177) came to the intriguing conclusion that 'pausin and verbalising one's problem-solving strategies impairs performance on insigh problems'. In fact, the authors point out that 'the present research suggests tha the relationship between language and thought is not always symbiotic', but tha 'in some situations language may interfere with thought'. Therefore, 'At least i the case of insight problems it may be better to "think before you speak"'.

Intuitive processing in the mind is only one area of the growing researc interest in this fascinating field. There is also the issue of how we perceive an acquire information. There is a recognition that conscious cognition may onl represent the tip of the iceberg in terms of the potential for the acquisitio of information. Lewicki *et al.* (1992: 796) express the view 'that nonconsciou information-acquisition processes are not only much faster but are als structurally more sophisticated in that they are capable of efficient processing o multidimensional and interactive relations between variables'.

'Most of the "real work", both in the acquisition of cognitive procedure and skills and in the execution of cognitive operations, such as encoding, an interpretation of stimuli, is being done at the level to which our consciousness ha

o access,' summarise Lewicki *et al.* (1992: 801), hinting at a vast terra incognita
lying behind the boundaries of the conscious domain which awaits exploration.
In the same vein, Claxton (1997: 144) points out that 'the fundamental design
specification of the unconscious neural biocomputer enables it to find, record
and use information that is of a degree of subtlety greater than we talk or think
about', again alluding at unexplored expanses, reminiscent of the oceans that are
still guarding most of their secrets.

While emphasising the role of intuition, it would be wrong, however, to swing
to the extreme in the sense of turning the tables on logic. Placing intuition instead
of logic in the seat of supremacy would appear a shortsighted continuation of
the domination-submission model of one overshadowing the other, instead of
initiating a model of peaceful coexistence in the sense of a true, constructive,
complementary and shared partnership along the lines of Poincaré's maxim: 'It is
by logic we prove, it is by intuition we discover'.

Franz Kafka's style of writing may serve as an example of such a model of
synergy between intuition and logic. As his biographer Citati (1990) concludes:

> His great novels are of an extreme complexity: a thousand relationships
> and internal connections run through them; an impression of an event is
> corrected, at a distance of hundreds of pages; every figure has only one
> meaning when counterposed to all the other figures; every sentence can be
> understood only if we set out from the totality of the book. So we would
> tend to believe that he laboriously drew up plans, projects, work schemes, or
> corrected and continually rearranged his book like Dostoevsky and Tolstoy.
> None of this is true. Down there, in the cellar, writing Amerika or The Trial or
> The Castle, Kafka did not even draft an outline or sketch: for him the problem
> of narrative architecture did not exist. Like a man possessed, he surrendered
> himself to the illimitable, wave-like imagination that flowed through him
> at night; and this nocturnal inspiration was endowed with all the structural
> knowledge he needed.
>
> Citati (1990: 56–57)

In this book, based on a pattern of self-observations, I have argued that m style of working represented an intuitive approach. Furthermore, I have argue that this intuitive approach could be defined as a method, as it was based on th self-organising dynamics of intuitive operations and processes taking shape i my mind.

Rather than surrendering to a particular type of thinking in terms c psychotherapeutic schools of thought, I gave my mind the freedom and autonom to follow its own processes, its own dynamics and laws of operation whil pursuing the discovery of childhood (post-)war trauma. In this sense, my learnin process did not consist of learning and assimilating lessons about particula schools of thought and of taking on board a procedural guidebook. In contras my learning process, which consisted of 'learning to unlearn' preconceived view about the operations of my mind, helped me to become aware of the mind enormous potential for discoveries about the early world of experience.

By writing about the marvels of intuition in this chapter I hope I hav succeeded in highlighting that the characteristic features and the flair of intuitiv operations, as they have been described by the series of personal accounts abov and by researchers, are very much identical to those I have experienced in th pursuit of my work. The fields of mathematics, physics, chemistry, medicine c psychotherapy may differ greatly in terms of their content; however, the 'facet of intuition' brought to bear in the process of discovery appear to be the sam as its wonders are rooted in the architecture of the brain.

Finally, the way in which I have presented the stories of the individuals in th book should not be taken as evidence for ascribing myself magic or 'guru'-lik abilities. My aim has simply been to draw attention to the inherent resources c the mind and to share my fascination with what they are capable of illuminatin provided they are given the space, the time and the mental attitude to displa their artistry.

CHAPTER 7

BETWEEN DESPAIR AND HOPE.
THE CHALLENGES OF PERCEPTION
AND PREVENTION

Nonetheless, the short lived triumph of the national socialist protest against anything existing is a reminder of how thin the layer can be between civilisation and barbarism.

Thamer, *Verführung und Gewalt*; my translation

They found that at least 9,796 civilians had lived through the fighting, surviving in the battlefield ruins. They included 994 children, of whom only nine were reunited with their parents. The vast majority were sent off to state orphanages or given work clearing the city.

Beevor, *Stalingrad*

CHILDREN IN CURRENT WARS

'"I was born in war," said one, "I have no home, no country and no friends, war is all my wealth and now whither shall I go?"' C. V. Wedgwood ([1938] 1992: 05) quotes a woman summarising the hopelessness of her existential situation t the end of the Thirty Years War in Germany in 1648. Twenty years earlier the prayer of Hartich Stiek, a peasant, remained unheard: 'God send that there may be an end at last: God send that there may be peace again. God in Heaven send us peace' (Wedgwood, [1938] 1992: 229).

Such outcries of despair, expressed more than three hundred years ago in Germany, were not condemned to history. They also occurred during the First World War, as is evident from Edith Hagener's moving account of her family (1986), and in the many wars that have taken place over the last half century.

After all, some wars – like that in Vietnam – dragged on for about thirty years, leaving a legacy like Bao Ninh's *The Sorrow of War* (1991) to remain in the hearts of those who had participated. Serving with the Glorious 27th Youth Brigade since 1969, Bao Ninh was one of five hundred men who went to war. When the war finally ended he was one of only ten who survived.

Wars and strife in countries with histories of conflicts lasting up to thirty years – such as in Angola, Afghanistan, Sri Lanka, Somalia and Sudan (UNICEF 1996) – have pushed these countries into an abyss. They depleted and plundered the coffers of the state – a pattern of war repeated throughout history (Kennedy 1989) – while filling the orphanages and undermining the path towards peace and prosperity. Although, at least in some parts of the world, the weaving of regional security arrangements appears to have tied down the paws of the war beast, it has clearly not been tamed. According to a 1996 UNICEF report, there have been 149 major wars between 1945 and 1992, with more than twenty-four million people killed. During 1995 alone the world experienced thirty armed conflicts. Such chilling facts emphasise that the topic of childhood war trauma has lost none of its urgency, none of its relevance and none of its poignancy. The need to care for war-traumatised children remains undiminished and the need to sensitise the global consciousness for the issues at stake is as great as ever.

> It has already been recognized (and provision has been made accordingly) that the lack of essential foods, vitamins, etc., in early childhood will cause lasting bodily malformation in later years, even if the harmful consequences are not immediately apparent. What is not yet generally recognized is that the same is true for the mental development of the child. Whenever certain

essential needs are not fulfilled, lasting psychological malformations will be the consequence; these essential elements are the need for personal attachment, for emotional stability, and for permanency of educational influence.

Burlingham and Freud (1942: 10)

In their study Dorothy Burlingham and Anna Freud described with admirable ucidity the impact of war on nursery children in London in 1942. Through their ioneering approach they laid the groundwork of awareness, observation, ntervention and, implicitly, prevention that has been the hallmark of more ecent studies.

Miljević-Ridjički's and Lugomer-Armano's study (1994) illustrates the mpact of war experiences on Croatian preschool children. 'War was clearly nd constantly in the children's minds' and 'War themes could be recognised n the children's verbal communication' are conclusions drawn from this study, vhich clearly demonstrates the powerful effect of the war events on these young hildren. 'Children are not isolated from the effects of warfare and understand far nore clearly than many adults would expect them to', is one of the key findings f their study, which I can confirm from my own observations, and which calls for nuch greater awareness and sensitivity for the plight of the younger generation.

Miljević-Ridjički and Lugomer-Armano (1994: 134) also make the important oint 'that the children [do] ... not merely reflect the grown-ups' comprehension f war, their answers clearly show that their concept of war is also based on their ersonal experience'. This demonstrates that the children were very much in ouch with the precious heartbeat of life. 'They clearly are emotionally involved nd would like the war to stop', conclude the authors (1994: 144), thus evoking he question of whether the world might be a more peaceful place if children had nore power to influence events − if only to prevent wars from erupting.

Ajduković (1996), while defining war-induced displacement as 'an intensely tressful experience', reports disturbing findings in a six-month follow-up study n war-displaced mothers and their children in Croatia. After a six-month eriod, nearly sixty percent of the children examined still displayed persistent

stress symptoms, the most persistent ones being aggression, separation fea
withdrawal, weeping and spitefulness. Even a year later, twelve percent of th
109 children studied still exhibited a range of five or more symptoms.

Displacement, with its concomitant stressful features of 'loss of famil
members and other important persons; traumatic events during flight, separatio
from parents and family, loss of home, living with distressed adults, los
educational opportunities and poor living conditions' (Ajduković and Ajduković
1993: 845–846) did not only affect the children but their mothers' behaviou
too. This is not surprising in view of the dreadful circumstances they foun
themselves in.

The results of Ajduković's study revealed 'that during displacement th
mothers' behaviour had become more unfavourable in two aspects: thes
mothers rarely talked to their children and were considerably more nervous. Th
number of mothers punishing their children more often was also higher' (199€
40) thus further compounding the problems for their children – so much so, i
fact, that Ajduković proposed that 'both displaced mothers and children ma
need additional psychosocial support or professional help' (1996: 47).

Stating that 'displacement and other related factors may have a lastin
impact on the development of some children', Ajduković (1996: 47) argued tha
'empowering mothers and encouraging them to develop constructive coping an
parenting skills could also help them to become more available, sensitive an
responsive to the needs of their children' (p. 47) surely a meaningful proposal i
view of the fact that there are 'currently more than 100.000 uprooted childre
in Croatia whose development is threatened due to unfavourable experience
in their lives and whose need for a supportive environment has increase€
(Ajduković, 1996: 36).

Croatia was not the only country drawn into the maelstrom of the war i
former Yugoslavia. There were also many Bosnian, Serbian and Albanian childre
who suffered immensely. A *Guardian* reporter painted this picture:

> It was one of the most poignant moments of the refugee exodus. Sitting
> solemn-faced behind the wheel of a tractor, his feet barely able to reach the

pedals a 10 year old boy steered his family across the Bosnian border into the safety of Serbia. His widowed mother, granny and 13 year old sister huddled in the trailer behind him. Their epic journey had covered 7 days and 800 war-torn kilometres since the Croats stormed into the Krajina village where they had lived. Miroslav was feted in the Serbian press as some kind of superhero, an icon of maturity, courage and resourcefulness.

But when Dr Veronica Ispanovic-Radojkovic, professor of child and adolescent psychiatry at Belgrade's Institute of Mental Health, saw him at a refugee centre a few days later, she found a sadly different reality. 'He was clearly depressive. He made no contact with other children and had great difficulties concentrating.'

Steele (26 August 1995: 25)

In a six-year follow-up study Sack and his co-workers (1993) reported their findings on Cambodian refugee adolescents who had experienced 'enormous ... war trauma ... over a 3 to 4 year period' at the hands of the Khmer Rouge. These traumas occurred while these children were between six and twelve years old and involved exposure to a gruesome spectrum of traumatic events ranging from loss of/or separation from parents to being interned in camps, beaten, tortured and threatened with being killed. 'For almost 4 years', Sack et al. commented, 'many lived under the daily threat of death: death by execution for stealing food or by starvation for not obtaining food' (1993: 435).

Given an observation period of six years, Sack and his co-workers found that post-traumatic stress disorder (PTSD) in these individuals persisted twelve years after the end of the traumatic events. Their study 'adds increasing empirical evidence to the finding that PTSD in children and adolescents persists' (1993: 436).

Although the Cambodian individuals had made successful adjustments to their new lives in the US, and although depressive symptoms appeared to have virtually disappeared over the observation period, there was further evidence for the long-term burden of the trauma experienced in the sense that 'PTSD continues to show a strong relationship to both resettlement stress and recent stressful events, suggesting that this diagnosis leaves one more vulnerable to th experience of subsequent stress' (Sack *et al.*, 1993: 437).

In his survey 'The Impact of Armed Conflict on Children' Onyango (1998 comes to similar grim conclusions. In countries with long histories of conflict 'an entire generation has grown up in the midst of war. Such people have know no peace at all' (Onyango, 1998: 219). Referring to UNICEF (1996) statistics, h pointed out that in the decade preceding 1998 'some 2–3 million children wer killed, while 4–5 million were disabled and a large number (more than a millior became orphans' (Onyango, 1998: 221). He concludes: 'This simply demonstrate that conflicts are not only capable of denying the children their right to surviv as guaranteed by the UN convention on the Rights of the Child but also denyin them the right to a family' (Onyango, 1998: 221).

While reviewing the problems armed conflicts cause to populations, suc as death and injury, displacement, life in camps, unaccompanied children an orphans, child soldiers and forced child workers, Onyango (1988) analyses th spectrum of negative consequences for children. Whereas the rate of malnutritio has been 'found to vary between 3% and 5% in various African countries, study conducted in 9 camps in Sudan found acute malnutrition among childre to be between 20% and 70%' (Onyango, 1998: 225). Equally worrying are th psychological effects on children, who are likely to have role model problem because the authority of parents may be undermined by a variety of causes. Th lack of education deprives children of their basic right to education and leave them in a trap of unfulfilled potential without proper skills.

There is also the disturbing impact of experienced violence on children' behaviour as 'conflicts expose children to a culture of violence, and most childre in such conditions grow up not having learnt how to respond to situation peacefully' (Onyango, 1998: 225). As such conditions may lead to a possibl perpetuation of the culture of violence, Taylor's (1998: 175) view deserve attention when he states that 'We need to learn more about how such traum causes later illness and behavioural disorders, lying dormant in the psyche t later spread as destructively as a latent virus.'

It is difficult to disagree with Onyango's (1998: 228) conclusion that 'the majority of the state parties to the international conventions, especially those in Africa, do very little to protect and care for children in situations of armed conflict'.

It is evident that this selection of studies about the traumatic impact of war on children portrays a depressing picture. At first sight, compared to the stories of German (post-)war children, the situation in terms of children's' exposure to war seems hardly changed. However, although there appears every reason to remain pessimistic, some subtle changes have taken place. They may be very small by comparison to the monstrosity of the spectrum of war-induced destruction. However, I feel it would be wrong to discount them completely.

By and large, 'early studies of children in war tended to emphasise their resilience in the face of extreme adversity' (Smith, 1998: 58). In more recent times, there has clearly been a growing awareness and more sophisticated perception of the psychological impact of war on children and of the psychological symptoms and disorders experienced.

This growth in perceptive awareness within the mental health profession has been astutely adressed by Yule *et al.* (1999: 25). Referring to a review by Garmezy and Rutter (1985), Yule and his co-workers conclude that 'focussing attention on resilience rather than pathology' was due to obtaining incomplete evidence because 'few investigations had done what is now so obvious – *they had not asked the children themselves!'* Yule and his co-workers continue their argument by stating that, 'it is really only in the past 15 years or so that traumatic stress reactions in children have been studied in a scientific, clinical manner'.

Despite there having been wars for thousands of years the development of professional awareness of war-induced suffering in children has taken rather longer and represents, in fact, a recent phenomenon. Awareness does, in effect, constitute an important professional tool because the recognition and study of a given psychological phenomenon depends on awareness. Once awareness has been generated, or possibly 'invented', it is likely to spark further interest. I suppose it is due to the creation of an awareness that the spark of interest in childhood war trauma has been ignited in many countries and many continents.

It is to be hoped that new directions of interest in terms of treatment strategies, facilities and training and research programmes will proliferate.

Over the last fifty years the issue of childhood war trauma has 'come of age'. From being very much a non-issue half a century ago, a body of interest and knowledge has developed since then. This has achieved at least one very important goal in terms of proving the harmful effect of war on children and their development.

It might also be worth noticing that the preoccupation with the issue of childhood war trauma is no longer restricted to the academic milieu. The involvement of international organisations, such as UNICEF, with their global appeal, demonstrates that the issue of childhood war trauma has been recognised as a global challenge, a challenge that transcends national boundaries and a challenge that aims at replacing the attitude of turning a blind eye to the fate of children in wartime with one that puts them and their suffering into the spotlight.

Of course, such an approach will not, in itself, prevent wars and it may not give children back their fathers, their mothers, their siblings, their relatives and friends, their homes, their country and, indeed, their innocence. However, the rise of an awareness may, in the end, prove the turning point towards strengthening the case for peace as a prerequisite for the healthy and protected development of children.

BUILDING BRIDGES.
HOLOCAUST AND (POST-)WAR TRAUMA IN CHILDHOOD

We appear normal, but no one can see our suffering.

Rachel Rubin, Holocaust survivor

Quoted in Boesch (2000)

Many years ago, while on a visit to 'my' beloved golden city of Prague, I attended the Jewish cemetery. Walking past the gravestones and looking at these lent testimonies, I reflected on the world of German and Czech Jewish life that ad once flourished until it was destroyed mercilessly. Later I entered a modest-ooking building on the compounds of the cemetery that had been converted into museum for all those children who were forcibly removed from their homes nd transported to the concentration camp in Theresienstadt. Here a deliberate ttempt was made to create an illusion of normality, while hiding the fact that he fate of all these children had already been sealed as part of the strategy – eliberately and coldly to annihilate the European Jewry. Eventually this was to aim the lives of the children in Theresienstadt, too. In the end, one and a half illion children perished in the Holocaust, making 'the fate of the children … many ways the most painful of all the tragedies of the Holocaust' (Gilbert, 987: 13).

Looking at the exhibits displayed in the museum, at the pictures of children nd at their drawings, I felt more than a sense of outrage, of incomprehension nd of shame about what happened in the country I belong to. Suddenly I felt very personal sense of attachment to these young children, boys and girls, ho were led towards their death not long before I was born, not too far from heresienstadt.

I knew that these young children were not my relatives, but I realised that hey could have been my friends at school or later at university. They could have een my colleagues. They could have been people whom I might have entrusted ith tasks of daily life or with the solution of complex problems. Their talents ight have brought insights, enrichments through art, or ideas and visions as o how to better the quality of the lives of human beings. As I said, none of the hildren I saw in front of me and whose anxieties and perceptions touched me ere relatives of mine.

I experienced a powerful feeling that it had not only been these children who ad been robbed of their lives. It seemed more. I realised that I, too, had been obbed of their precious lives. Leaving the museum, the feeling that my friends ad been murdered stayed with me.

Years later, in the summer of the year 2000, I was invited to take part in a panel iscussion during a conference in London entitled 'Remembering for the Future'.

This conference was devoted to a whole range of issues related to the Holocaust. I was very moved by this invitation. When I took my seat on the panel, I was surrounded by colleagues who had escaped the Holocaust as Kindertransportees and when I looked into the audience there were a great number of people who likewise had escaped the Nazi terror as Kindertransportees.

I had not been able to talk to the children whose memory is preserved at the museum attached to the Jewish cemetery in Prague. However, it was possible to start to talk to my various colleagues on the panel. There was a sense of building bridges, not with expensive bricks, cement or steel but through the help of different, yet miraculous 'commodities' such as words, feelings and shared perceptions that left me with the belief in the importance of continuing with the process of fostering understanding between humans traumatised by the Holocaust and those traumatised by war.

Although wishing to make an observation, I do not want to create the impression that I am an expert on the issue of the Holocaust. Over the years, substantial amount of research has been carried out and there is hardly anything I could contribute. My observation is simply meant to be a personal one inspired by the idea of building bridges of understanding.

Children who suffered in the Holocaust were the victims of genocide and the children who suffered in the Second World War were the victims of actions of war. It is not my intention to compare these two kinds of sufferings in any way and I do not think that they can be compared. War between military opponents and genocide are different issues. The latter breaks all the rules and respect for human rights and is unleashed against wholly defenceless citizens, adults, children and the elderly and executed through ruthless deception to the very end.

However, looking at the consequences it appears to me that there are similarities that may merit attention. Both the Holocaust and the Second World War ended at about the same time. This ending does, however, only represent an end in a historical sense. As far as the (post-)war children are concerned their suffering has continued to this day. Likewise the tragedy of the children of the Holocaust Martin Gilbert refers to did not cease in 1945. It is not a tragedy ssigned to the past. The lives of those who survived the Holocaust, and in articular the lives of those who survived the Holocaust as children, have been ffected by this tragedy to this day through wounds that have never healed.

Mazor and colleagues (1990), for instance, studied the long-term psychological onsequences due to childhood trauma of Holocaust survivors forty years later. Vhat they found in their non-clinical group of subjects was that

> it was only when they were about 50 years old that they opened up and attempted to give a historical meaning to life. When this process takes place, it is possible to discover the depths of their wounds. Moreover there are dimensions that remain painful and untouched and were not transformed, such as feelings towards persecutors ...
>
> Mazor *et al.* (1990: 11–12)

The finding that such deep wounds persisted is the more poignant as all the ndividuals in this study 'have proved their strength and coping ability despite a estructive past and loss ... All the individuals ... succeeded in accomplishing heir life tasks ... and, in addition, most of them participated in establishing the tate of Israel' (Mazor *et al.*, 1990: 11).

However, the degree of coping appears not to be a reliable guide as to he presence or absence of psychological wounds. This aspect is emphasised y Sadavoy, who states: 'The more convincing data suggested that emotional eactivity often may remain intense and dysphoric without affecting measures of daptation and overt behaviour' (1996: 290).

Sadavoy makes the important point that

> the idea that deeper psychological problems may remain hidden unless specifically sought out is illustrated by Matussek (1961). Writing about 130 patients who were believed to show no after-effects of the concentration camp experience, he (Matussek) observed that, on closer inquiry, he did not see a single person in this group who was without pathology.
>
> Sadavoy (1996: 290)

187

The unsuspecting observer may be misguided in coming to the conclusion that everything appears normal while in reality the suffering continues unabated giving credence to Rachel Rubin's comment quoted above. While children who survived the Holocaust and children who suffered (post-)war trauma may have coped well and successfully in subsequent life, these findings suggest that the conclusion of psychological well-being can only be drawn, if at all, after very careful and perceptive examination.

This is supported by a study of Robinson *et al.* (1994) from the Center for Research into the Late Effects of the Holocaust in Jerusalem who interviewed 100 Holocaust survivors who suffered from Nazi persecution during their childhood years. Even fifty years after the trauma the survivors suffered from a whole range of significant psychological and psychosomatic problems, such as nervousness, insomnia, nightmares with Holocaust content, headaches, depression, anxiety, survivor guilt, to name just some of the symptoms listed by the above authors.

Time has appeared to be no healer, and thus the authors conclude:

> that the after-effects of massive prolonged trauma in childhood may persist for an entire lifetime. The more massive the trauma, the more severe its after-effects. Children who endured massive and prolonged trauma may reveal symptoms of post-traumatic stress disorder for many years.
>
> Robinson *et al.* (1994: 245)

In addition to the range of symptoms described in the Robinson *et al.* (1994) study there is the impact of a massive trauma on early development. Sadavoy (1996) notion of a traumatically induced 'false self' highlights the extent to which the massive trauma hinders proper emotional development. He argues that the 'false self' may be interpreted as 'effective coping skills that are observed in many survivors'. The 'false self ... may be conceptualised as a form of character armour, protecting the victim's true self that was impinged upon by the trauma'. What Sadavoy in effect describes may be seen as an identity disorder, in which the 'false self meets the world successfully', while 'the traumatically affected part of the (true) self lies vulnerable beneath the surface'. In effect, it is the lying eneath the surface which renders the true, but vulnerable self the dominant ɔrce in emotional life because it imposes 'the need to live a pleasureless life ... rovoking unusual fears of separation, inner feelings of emptiness predisposing ɔ depression ... and intense longing for those who were lost' (Sadovoy, 1996: 95).

The value of the 'false self' concept lies in resolving the contradiction ꞏetween an apparently normal adjustment and the persistence of deep wounds nd vulnerabilities. This aspect, however, is not unique to Holocaust survivors. ꞏs I have observed, it is found in (post-)war-traumatised children as well.

Returning to the issue of shared aspects of the Holocaust and (post-)war rauma I will now refer to the extent to which the impact of the trauma has ffected the second generation of Holocaust survivors; this has been movingly lustrated in the work of Wardi (1992). What appears to have happened is that ne experience of the intensity of the psychosocial trauma rendered the mothers ncapable of perceiving their children appropriately due to 'a considerable ognitive distortion of their [i.e. mothers'] perception of the child's true essence' Wardi, 1992: 30). One of the individuals described provides an illuminating ccount of her mother having looked after her in a manner as if she was a 'china ꞏoll' ... and thus 'always nice, neat, pretty, well-dressed and well-tended' (Wardi, 992: 75). What was missing in her mother's approach, however, was the crucial ngredient of perception due to, in Wardi's words 'the mother's ... inability to feel ꞏer daughter's emotions' (Wardi, 1992: 76). It is this lack of emotional perception nd sensitivity, and the psychological environment of emotional fatherlessness r motherlessness, that countless (post-)war children share.

Furthermore, both Holocaust and (post-)war children share the fate of having ꞏad to live in a social environment that was, at least initially, far from perceptive ɔ their suffering. It took time and the development of a new professional wareness and sensitivity to create the basis for an understanding which paid ribute to the depth and complexities of their suffering. Until the early 1980s, as ꞏestenberg (1998) points out, the traumas of Holocaust victims in the US were ꞏardly touched on in the course of psychoanalytical treatments. However, since ꞏen, there has been a growing process of perception, as far as the psychological implications of Holocaust trauma are concerned. By contrast, by and large, the former (post-)war children are still experiencing a lack of professional perception of the traumatic issues at stake and of their long-ranging effects.

Creating a professional awareness of the spectrum and of the scale of problems faced by Holocaust survivors required human perception and an independent line of thinking that was prepared to sacrifice dogmatic view wherever necessary, in order not to lose sight of the splintered worlds of the sufferers. Likewise, for instance, courage and vision were required to build bridge of understanding between children of Holocaust survivors and children of Nazi perpetrators (Bergmann *et al.*, 1998, Bar-On, 2000).

Yet the effort to break the wall of silence and to overcome preconceived notions in order to have a clearer view of the human dimension of suffering appears to have been more than worthwhile. 'Supporting each other through this learning process has proved to be tremendously helpful and may well be the only way to prevent trauma from being passed on to the following generations, states Goschalk (2000: 47) in 'A Challenge to my World-View', the essence of her experience in a group of participants of Jewish, Palestinian and German background who had gathered 'To reflect and trust'.

I hope I have been able to convince the reader that I do not want to draw comparisons between the sufferings resulting from childhood (post-)war trauma and those due to the genocidal horror of the Holocaust. In my view, each victim has the right to be recognised and respected in accordance with the extent of the suffering endured. By drawing attention to what appear to me certain similarities in terms of aspects of trauma experienced by those who were traumatised by the Holocaust and those who suffered (post-)war trauma in childhood, it has been my aim to create a broader basis of mutual understanding, to help to alleviate the sense of loneliness of suffering, and to alert the professional perception towards realising the mountains of unseen suffering still filling the landscapes of memories more than five decades later.

The number of houses and bridges that had to be rebuilt after the end of the Second World War was staggering. This task was completed in a relatively short space of time. However, even half a century after the end of the Second World

War it is becoming ever more apparent how many invisible bridges still have to
e rebuilt — bridges made of trust, of sensitivity, of tact, of respect and of hope.
seems to me that the task has hardly begun.

CHILDHOOD WITHOUT WAR.
A UTOPIAN DREAM?

*In the South Atlantic Ocean, the explorer Ernest Shackleton, after two years of
isolation in the remote Antarctic, finally reached the small island of South Georgia.
In his memoirs he recalled his first question to Mr Sorlle, the manager of the tiny
British whaling station there, and Sorlle's reply:*
'Tell me, when was the war over?' I asked.
*'The war is not over,' he answered 'Millions are being killed. Europe is mad. The
world is mad.'*

Gilbert, *The First World War*

My son was killed while laughing at some jest.
I would I knew
What it was and it might serve me in a time
When jests are few.

Kipling about the death of his only son, John,
killed during the battle of Loos in September 1915

'They wanted peace and they fought for thirty years to be sure of it. They
id not learn then, and have not since, that war breeds only war,' concludes
. V. Wedgwood ([1938] 1992: 526) in her epic account of the Thirty Years War
hich devastated Germany between 1618 and 1648 amidst the war-torn world of
eventeenth-century Europe. These last sentences of C. V. Wedgwood's account

could hardly have been more prophetic. Barely a year after the first publication of her book the Second World War broke out and this, in turn, happened barely twenty years after the end of the First World War.

If there are lessons to be learnt from the fates of (post-)war children described in this book then they surely have to be concerned with the prevention of wars. There is a well-established principle in medicine and mental health which demands prevention, once the cause of a particular kind of damage has been recognised and established. This principle needs to be applied rigorously to the issue of (post-)war childhood trauma in order to prevent future damage of future generations and to alleviate the suffering that has already been afflicted.

This demands actions to be taken beyond the traditional medical sphere of influence. Of course, prevention of further wars has to be initiated by policy initiatives and an effective framework of international law in order to curb the destructive power of fervent nationalism, religious fanaticism, racial superiority, excessive militarism, and to strengthen effective democratic structures and security arrangements.

However, as there has been such long-standing failure throughout the centuries to perceive the suffering of children through war, mental health professionals have to raise their voices and have to make a contribution towards the formulation of anti-war policies.

Furthermore, I believe there have to be educational initiatives in order to mobilise support for preventative measures. These would, for instance, involve teaching children at an early age to grasp the factors that lead to wars, to teach them the horrific impact of wars on people's lives and to help them assimilate a value system based on the appreciation of peace, built on mutual tolerance and respect for the diversity of cultures, ethnicities, religious aspirations and individuality.

Dismantling authoritarian influences in family life, education and the social environment, would, at least in my view, have to be part of a preventative programme. There is sufficient evidence to suggest that authoritarian influences are likely to inflict psychological damage on children. Emotional pressure and fear imposed by authority figures are liable to stunt the emotional growth of hildren, their self-esteem and their striving towards individual thinking. Alice Miller's (1981) eloquent psycho-historical account, *For Your Own Good: Roots of Violence in Child-rearing,* provides ample evidence for the damaging impact of the authoritarian 'philosophy' that runs counter to any modern understanding of the requirements for children's enlightened development.

It is presumably not a a coincidence that three of Germany's greatest writers of the last century suffered the excesses of what I call authoritarian abuse, either at home or at school. These were: Franz Kafka, Rainer Maria Rilke and Robert Musil. In his *Brief an den Vater* [Letter to the father] Franz Kafka, the great prophet of the dictatorial apocalypse that was to befall Germany, provided a heartbreaking account of his struggle with the figure of his authoritarian father.

Writing about the 'daily despair of a ten, twelve, fourteen year old boy', Rainer Maria Rilke, the wonderful poet, recalled his intense suffering during his years of attendance at a military college for boys in St. Pölten in Austria (1920b: 7). Eventually leaving the school 'exhausted and as someone who had been physically and mentally abused', he described the sheer misery of his experience in terms suggestive of a psychotrauma that would have prevented him from realising his life the way he had fulfilled it, had he not 'suppressed ... for decades .. all the memories' of his 'five years of education at the military establishment' (Rilke, 1920b: 17).

Robert Musil, the creator of the famous epic *The Man Without Qualities,* weaves into his novel *Die Verwirrungen des Zöglings Törleß* aspects of his own disturbing experiences at a military college in Moravia which he entered at the age of fourteen years. Musil's biographer, Berghahn, in his analysis of the deeper layers of meaning in this novel, wrote:

> Without knowing, Musil describes the history preceding the dictatorships of the 20th century. He illuminates the psychological tensions and the sexual aggressions of some adolescents in the seclusion of a military school and traces the whole arsenal of brutalities that were to make history later on ... Underneath the surface of foolish actions of the pupils, barbarism breaks through. Eventually, cruelty committed by youth reveals the methods of a

concentration camp. And yet it is a famous and exclusive institution where all this happens.

Berghahn (1963: 28–29); my translation

Even forty years after his school days it was with horror that Robert Mus remembered the military school in which the pupils were kept like prisoners describing it with uncharacteristic bluntness as the 'arsehole of the devil'.

These were writers with sensitivity to the hidden currents of socia developments, with the gift of reflecting personal experiences within the mirror of the social context, and with a genius for finding words to express the abus suffered at the hands of the authoritarian culture. However, they were not alone Scientists, too, recognised the profound and damaging flaws of the authoritaria culture. Describing the impact of the authoritarian education on the young Alber Einstein, his biographer Wickert (1972) stated that:

> The method of inducing anxiety, the force and the false authority did, however, take away from the pupil Einstein any joy of the school and the various topics. Later in life Albert Einstein stated that one tried 'to strangle the joy, the holy curiosity of the searching mind; for this delicate little plant requires stimulating encouragement and most importantly freedom'.

Wickert (1972: 9–10); my translation

The depth of perception and the creative genius of these outstanding gifted individuals protected them from surrendering their individuality to th authoritarian code of blind obedience, from submission and from sacrificin their individual set of values. However, history has provided ample evidenc of the extent to which such an authoritarian code, whether exemplified b the figurehead of an emperor like Wilhelm II or by Hitler's 'Führer'-principle contains a very real risk of war. In such a system, the man at the top of th authoritarian pyramid is capable of starting wars virtually at will by the push of button, without there being sufficient controls to check such actions.

Ian Kershaw's (1991) brilliant anatomy of the fascist dictatorship in Germany that is based on Max Weber's concept of 'charismatic domination' implicitly illustrates the underlying weakness and vulnerability of a society whose intrinsic authoritarian system provided the breeding ground for the spreading of the very virus of obedience and submission that, in the end, was to destroy it.

Since 1945 there have been further examples of wars having been started by dictators operating at will within authoritarian environments. Therefore, dismantling authoritarian systems and ideologies appears a necessary preventative step in order to reduce the risk of wars. Of course, such a task involves more than policy initiatives at an adult level. In my view, encouraging children from early on in life to became aware of their own self-worth, of their own emotional sophistication, of their own wonders of thinking, and of the importance of exploring and conceptualising the world with their own mind, represents more than a strategy towards enhancing the psychological development and welfare of children. It also represents a strategy of war prevention because the shield of individuality and of independent feeling and thinking will provide a protection against such mindless battle cries as those of a promised land lasting a thousand years that collapsed totally after only twelve.

Undoubtedly, there would have been no First World War if there had been more perceptive and independent-minded individuals such as the brilliant German industrialist Albert Ballin. Outraged by the outbreak of the war in 1914, he openly and fearlessly accused the German Chancellor von Bethmann-Hollweg of being responsible for the terrible misery and the death of hundreds of thousands of people (Wiborg, 1998). Already in the autumn of 1914, describing the war as the 'most stupid and most bloody the world history has ever seen' (Wiborg, 1998: 15), Ballin pleaded passionately for an end to the war and for a peace agreement. His pleas, however, fell on deaf ears. Ironically, years later, it was Ballin, the 'pacifist' who was asked to convey the fact to the German Kaiser that the war had been lost. None of the military leaders who had shown so much 'courage' to send millions to their death had the guts to explain this very fact to the Kaiser.

Reading the portraits of German military leaders in Barnett's *Hitler's Genera* (1995), one wonders whether there might not have been a Second World Wa if the majority of these military leaders had not been equipped with mindset indoctrinated by authoritarian principles that rendered them susceptible t 'charismatic domination'. And one might wonder whether there would hav been a Second World War if more German soldiers had followed the exampl of Barbara Meter's (1996) father who shot in the air instead of aiming at th 'enemy'.

> The indictment implied not only that he had acted on purpose, which he did not deny, but out of base motives and in the full knowledge of the criminal nature of his deeds. As for the base motives, he was perfectly sure that he was not what he called an innerer Schweinehund, a dirty bastard at heart; and as for his conscience, he remembered perfectly well that he would have had a bad conscience only if he had not done what he had been ordered to do — to ship millions of men, women and children to their death with great zeal and the most meticulous care.
>
> Arendt (1994: 25)

It is with these words that Hannah Arendt characterises Adolf Eichmann, key figure in the Holocaust, the incarnation of the 'Banality of Evil', who state that 'he had always been a law-abiding citizen, because Hitler's orders, which h had certainly executed to the best of his ability, had possessed the "force of law in the Third Reich', and a man who denied ever having 'killed a Jew or a non-Jev and who 'left no doubt that he would have killed his own father if he had receive an order to that effect' (Arendt, 1994: 22).

Is it permitted to speculate that Hannah Arendt's indictment is more than th indictment of an individual? Can it also be interpreted as a powerful indictmer of the supreme command of the authoritarian code — namely, to obey orders Has she not exposed the dimension lurking carefully hidden behind this suprem command — namely, brutal inhumanity?

Again, is one allowed to speculate whether the Holocaust would have taken place if there had been more people resisting orders? More people challenging the perversion of the term 'duty', as it was defined by Heinrich Himmler who used a 'trick' (Arendt, 1994: 106): 'So that instead of saying: What horrible things I did to people!, the murderers would be able to say: What horrible things had to watch in pursuance of my duties, how heavily the task weighed on my shoulders!'

However, banishing the ghosts of the authoritarian heritage cannot be the only goal. Considerable efforts are being made of enabling the next generation of children to benefit from the revolution in information technology sweeping the globe. Therefore it seems to me that the time has come to spread the knowledge of another, no less important revolution amongst the next generation. I am referring to the psychological revolution that has enormously deepened the understanding of early human development. Initiated by Sigmund Freud a century ago, it has been gathering pace over the last fifty years, particularly fuelled by John Bowlby's (1971) work on attachment and the growing field of infant research. This revolution has defined the conditions children require to attain a sound and stable basis for the formation of their personality and future.

Unfortunately, however, the wealth of knowledge accumulated has not spread sufficiently into schools and families. Creating the climate for this would again constitute a preventative step against war. Whoever has experienced in his own childhood the immense value of positive conditions for growth is unlikely to want to risk losing them through the folly of war.

I suggest that prevention strategies geared towards changing social behaviour, and the dissemination of psychological knowledge into educational and family settings, have to be priorities in an increasingly global 'village' in order to reduce the risk of war flames charring the hopes and aspirations of future generations.

In presenting the findings I have described in this book it has been my intention to draw attention to the wide range of polytraumas caused by the impact of the Second World War and its aftermath on (post-)war children. From the detached observer's point of view the psychological damage inflicted by war on children represents all that is damaging for children in terms of emotional trauma, deprivation of growth-enhancing structures, interference with th formation of their personality, self-esteem and potential. There can be no doub that war represents a cruel and often irreversible harm to the well-being of th most vulnerable members of society, often turning them into lifelong victims.

Such experiments have to stop. For all too long children's sufferings in war have not been noticed nor taken care of. For all too long the attitude toward children has been dominated by a notion of adult superiority such as the on reflected in the response of King Philip II of France in the thirteenth centur when 'Stephen, aged twelve, led a crowd of 30,000 into Paris ... in a children' crusade' (Rosen, 1994: 21):

> My child, you claim to serve God's natural order better than we do, but you
> are mistaken. For in this order parents command children, priests bless,
> knights fight, peasants labour and children obey. If we let children preach and
> command, do you not see that the order is reversed? The devil has led you
> into a trap and you have fallen into it.
>
> Rosen (1994: 21)

Maybe after so many centuries the time has come to challenge this orde and to establish a new order in which the supremacy of obedience is ende and in which children are given an equal place, an equal status, an equal degre of respect in society, and a share of the power to shape and to possibly vet developments such as wars that they know are harmful.

The emergence of the environmental movement has catalysed a ne consciousness about the relationship between humans and the plane Sustainable development is a term that is based on an attitude of replacin exploitation, destruction and blindness towards the environment by an approac of perceiving and respecting the conditions for maintaining a healthy equilibriu and availability of resources for future generations.

Similarly, a new awareness and political initiatives are required, based on green 'environmental psychology' of establishing, securing and fostering optimur conditions for children's psychological and physical growth. The attitude c

ominance, of suppression and of superiority in respect of children needs to
e discarded. Wars are the reflection of a way of 'old thinking', of perceptive
lindness towards children. Peace is required to provide the framework for
table, reliable, protective conditions for children to develop.

The Greek saying, 'War is the father of all things', echoes through European
nd German history. In Germany the Thirty Years War, the Seven Years War, the
irst World War, the Second World War (to name but a few), and the war against
ewish Citizens, the Holocaust, suggest that the time has come to reflect on new
riorities.

Maybe the time has come to say: 'Peace is the father of all things'. And maybe
t would be an even more imaginative break with the past mode of thinking to
ay: 'Children are the father and future of all things'.

Maybe in ten, maybe in a hundred, or maybe in a thousand years, a world
may have been realised where Robert Musil's (1952) 'Möglichkeitssinn' [sense
f possibilities] has acquired the same status as a 'Wirklichkeitssinn' [sense of
eality], where logical reason and intuition are complementary and mutually
upportive expressions of the mind; where children and adults are equal partners,
eing variations of one and the same and where wars are distant sorrows of the
ast. Then Isaiah's (2: 4) prophesy will have come true, where 'nation shall not
ft up sword against nation, neither shall they learn war anymore'.

SPLINTERED INNOCENCE

Men with cold hearts and golden swords
forget the innocent: 'us' the younger generations

Cold kisses float in the dismal air
Bare limbs rattle in the wind
No houses live. Gardens die
Innocence drifts in the smoky breeze
Small boys pick up crushed toys
Small girls with no smile
Dead bodies lie in the sunlight
No name echoes. Just limp like bare trees
Relatives weep. Hearts break
Time stops

Fingers touch
Love neglected
Letters missed
Age is twisted
Cuts bleed. Tears roll
Sadness lingers in the thick shadowy nights

Days roll on
Life is sliced
Pureness seeps
Dust and despair prevail
Birds twitter
Separation burns

Nothing heals
The pain, the pain
Of endless days
Of endless wars
Of endless scars

Just dead

If only it would
If only it would
Babies would be babies
Children children
Mothers mothers
Fathers fathers
Uncles uncles

Lives could live
Rather than be buried
Being buried for heartless wars
For heartless strife

The innocent now want a voice
No longer be harmed
No longer be suffering
No longer be threatened
No longer be splintered

Splintered into smithereens
Without care for them
Washed away with the tide

Just stop. Stop it now
Before we all succumb to this plague
The plague of war

Before we all fade into abandoned ashes

Before we are splintered
Splintered into non-existence

Ana Sophia Sawaya Heinl
For all of those who have suffered due to these bloody, bloody wars

TIMELESS GRATITUDE

Härte schwand. Auf einmal legt sich Schonung
an der Wiesen aufgedecktes Grau.
Kleine Wasser ändern die Betonung.
Zärtlichkeiten, ungenau
 Rainer Maria Rilke
 Vorfrühling

Toughness ceased. And mercy that once faltered
now covers the meadows' erstwhile grey.
And, drop by drop, the emphasis is altered.
Tenderness delicately now holds sway
 Rainer Maria Rilke
 Vorfrühling, translated by B. Green

To my parents in gratitude for life and survival in dark times.
To an unknown Czech doctor and a Hungarian messenger in gratitude for support in
1945.
To an American family for sending me CARE parcels.
To my children in gratitude for allowing me to relive the experience of childhood in
more peaceful times.
To Anabelle for growing roses in the desert.

BIBLIOGRAPHY

The real war will never get in the books.

Walt Whitman, 1875

The list of references is meant to be an introductory one. My main aim has ,een to include those books that I found helpful, thought-provoking or moving.
= I were to single out some books in relation to German (post-)war children that ?ade a particularly profound impression on me – and I am very much aware that his is an entirely subjective matter – they would include Gerhard Gronefeld's ?mall book of children's photographs. Although complemented by a German ext, the touching and powerful photographs speak for themselves, transcending he barrier of language. Hauschild and Umbehr's photo documentary provides he example of a book illustrating the reality of living conditions for refugee hildren in (post-)war Germany. I also recommend Robert Capa's outstanding hoto documentary about Berlin shortly after the capitulation. Apart from being powerful indictment of war, Capa's photographs convey the urban apocalypse nfolding in front of the eyes of (post-)war children living and growing up in ?erlin.

When it comes to a description of the totality of the senseless brutality of ?ar from an adult perspective and its implicit indirect impact on children, then rich Maria Remarque's classic *All Quiet on the Western Front*, Antony Beevor's nique account of the battle of Stalingrad, and Bao Ninh's *The Sorrow of War* ?e essential reading.

With respect to intuition, I found Guy Claxton's *Hare Brain Tortoise Mind* xciting reading.

Ajduković, M. (1996) Mothers' perception of their relationship with their children during displacement: a six-months follow-up. Child Abuse Review, 5: 34–49.

Ajduković, M. and Ajduković, D. (1993) Psychological well-being of refugee children. Child Abuse & Neglect, 17 (6): 843–854.

Arad, Y. (ed.) (1990) The Pictorial History of the Holocaust. Jerusalem: Yad Vashem.

Arendt, H. (1994) Eichmann in Jerusalem. A report on the Banality of Evil. London: Penguin.

Ariès, Ph. (1996) Centuries of Childhood. London: Pimlico.

Atkinson, L. (2000) Trusting your own judgement (for allowing yourself to eat the pudding), in T. Atkinson and G. Claxton (ed.), The Intuitive Practicioner. On the Value of Not Always Knowing What One is Doing. Buckingham: The Open University Press.

Baker, R. (ed.) (1983) The Psychosocial Problems of Refugees. London: The British Refugee Council.

Barnett, C. (ed.) (1995) Hitler's Generals. London: Phoenix.

Bar-On, Dan (ed.) (2000) Bridging the Gap: Storytelling as a Way to Work Through Political and Collective Hostilities. Hamburg: Edition Körber-Stiftung.

Bauby, J. D. (1997) The Diving-Bell and the Butterfly. London: Fourth Estate.

Beevor, A. (1998) Stalingrad. London: Viking.

Benn, G. quoted from the poem 'Du mußt Dir alles geben …', in W. Lenning (1962) Benn. Hamburg: Rowohlt.

Berghahn, W. (1963) Robert Musil. Hamburg: Rowohlt.

Bergmann, M. S. and Jucovy, M. E. (ed.) (1982) Generations of the Holocaust. New York: Basic Books.

Bergmann, M. S., Jucovy, M. E. and Kestenberg, J. S. (ed.) (1998) Kinder der Opfer, Kinder der Täter. Frankfurt am Main: Fischer.

Boesch, J. P. (2000) Survivors of the Holocaust … Today. Gollion: Infolio.

Bohart, A. C. (1999) Intuition and creativity in psychotherapy. Journal of Constructivist Psychology, 12: 287–311.

Bowlby, J. (1971) Attachment and Loss, Volume 1, Attachment. Harmondsworth: Penguin.

Brian, D. (1996) Einstein, A Life. John Wiley & Sons: New York.

Buchheim, L. G. (1996) The Boat. London: Cassell.

urlingham, D. and Freud, A. (1942) Young Children in War-time. A Year's Work in a Residential War Nursery. London: George Allen & Unwin.

apa, R. (1986) Sommertage, Friedenstage, Berlin 1945. Kreuzberg: Dirk Nishen.

itati, P. (1990) Kafka. London: Martin Secker & Warburg.

laxton, G. (1997) Hare Brain Tortoise Mind: Why Intelligence Increases when you Think less. London: Fourth Estate.

laxton, G. (2000) The anatomy of intuition, in T. Atkinson and G. Claxton (ed.). The Intuitive Practitioner. On the Value of Not Always Knowing What One is Doing. Buckingham: The Open University Press.

eich, F. (1962) Windarzt und Apfelsinenpfarrer. Freiburg: Herder.

ollinger, H. (ed.) (1983) Kain, wo ist dein Bruder? Frankfurt am Main: Büchergilde Gutenberg.

ombrowski, E., Kraus E. und Schramm, K. (1965) Wie es war. Mainzer Schicksalsjahre 1945–1948. Mainz: Mainzer Verlagsanstalt.

asterbrook, J. A. (1959) The effect of emotion on cue utilization and the organization of behaviour. Psychological Review, 66: 183–201.

insiedel Heinrich Graf von (1984) The Onslought. The German Drive to Stalingrad. London: Sidgwick & Jackson.

oreman, M. (1991) War Boy. London: Puffin.

riedrich, O. (1996) The Kingdom of Auschwitz. London: Penguin.

riesen, A. von (2000) Der lange Abschied. Psychische Spätfolgen für die 2. Generation deutscher Vertriebener. Gießen: Edition Psychosozial.

röhling, U. (1991) Die langen Schatten der Kindheit. Hamburg: Brigitte, 11: 118–124.

allaz, Ch. (1985) Rose Blanche. London: Cape.

ieve, Th. (1997) Es gibt hier keine Kinder. There are no children here. Auschwitz, Groß-Rosen, Buchenwald. Göttingen: Wallstein.

ilbert, M. (1987) The Holocaust. The Jewish Tragedy. London: Fontana Press.

ilbert, M. (1994) The First World War. London: Weidenfeld & Nicolson.

ilbert, M. (2000) Never Again. A History of the Holocaust. London: HarperCollins.

oethe, Johann Wolfgang von, quoted in Musil, R. (1952) Der Mann ohne Eigenschaften. Hamburg: Rowohlt.

Goschalk, J. C. (2000) A Challenge to my world-view. Reflecting the personal processes during TRT-Work, in D. Bar-On (ed.), Bridging the Gap. Hamburg: Edition Körber-Stiftung.

Gronefeld, G. (1985) Kinder nach dem Krieg. Berlin: Dirk Nishen.

Grube, F. und Richter G. (1980) Flucht und Vertreibung. Deutschland zwischen 1944 und 1947. Hamburg: Hoffmann & Campe.

Hadamard, J. (1949) The Psychology of Invention in the Mathematical Field. Princeton: Princeton University Press.

Hagener, E. (1986) Es lief sich so sicher an Deinem Arm. Weinheim: Beltz

Handke, P. (2000) Sorrow Beyond Dreams. London: Pushkin Press.

Härtling, P. (1980) Nachgetragene Liebe. Darmstadt: Luchterhand.

Hauschild, W. und Umbehr, O. (1985) Im Flüchtlingslager 1947/48. Berlin: Dirk Nishen.

Heinl, A. S. S. (2000) Splintered Innocence. Unpublished poem.

Heinl, H. (1984) Feldpostbriefe. Integrative Therapie, 4, Paderborn: Junferman.

Heinl, P. (1987a) The image and visual analysis of the geneogram. Journal of Family Therapy, 7: 213–229.

Heinl, P. (1987b) Visual geneogram work and change: a single case study. Journal of Family Therapy, 9: 281–291.

Heinl, P. (1987c) The interactional sculpt: examples from a training seminar. Journal of Family Therapy, 9: 189–198.

Heinl, P. (1988) Object sculpting, symbolic communication and early experience: a single case study. Journal of Family Therapy, 10: 167–178.

Heinl, P. (1991) Therapie im sprachlosen Raum: HWS-Trauma in der Kindheit. Praxis der Psychotherapie und Psychosomatik, Springer Verlag, 36: 324–330.

Heinl, P. (1994a) "Maikäfer flieg, dein Vater ist im Krieg, ..." Seelische Wunden aus der Kriegskindheit. München: Kösel.

Heinl, P. (1994b) Kriegskindheitstraumatisierungen, in I. Olbricht and M. Wernado (ed.) Wertewandel in einer sich wandelnden Welt. Schmallenberg: Grobbel.

Heinl, P. (1997) Kriegsblindheit. Psychologie in der Medizin, 1: 32–34.

Heinl, P. (1998) Sich selbst organisierendes Denken in der Exploration früher familiensystemischer Erfahrungen. Systhema 1: 44–55.

einl, P. (1999) Kriegskindheitstraumata: Die Splitter in unverheilten Wunden und die Herausforderung für das Bewußtsein der Zukunft, in B. Heller (ed.), Maikäfer flieg, dein Vater war im Krieg. Hofgeismar: Evangelische Akademie.

einl, P. (2000) The infant voice in adult speech: the transmission of information about the first year of life in adult communication. Intl. J. Prenatal and Perinatal Psychology and Medicine, 12 (1): 155–166.

einl, P. (2001) Die Rosen des Verstehens. Seminarprogramm der Bildungsstätte Soonwald Schlösschen.

ersey, J. (1946) Hiroshima. London: Penguin.

odges, A. (1992) Alan Turing. The Enigma. London: Vintage.

offman, P. (1998) The Man Who Loved Only Numbers. The Story of Paul Erdös and the Search for Mathematical Truth. London: Fourth Estate.

olmes, R. (2009) The Second World War in Photographs. London: Carlton Books.

ousden, R. and Goodchild, C. (ed.) (1992) We Two. Couples Talk About Living, Loving and Working Partnerships for the '90s. London: Aquarian Press.

ürgens-Kirchhoff, A. (1993) Schreckensbilder. Krieg und Kunst im 20. Jahrhundert. Berlin: Reimer.

afka, F. (1999) Brief an den Vater. Frankfurt am Main: Fischer.

anigel, R. (1992) The Man who knew Infinity. A Life of the Genius Ramanujan. London: Abacus.

arpov, V. (1987) Russia at War, 1941-45. London: Stanley Paul.

eegan, J. (1976). The Face of Battle. London: Penguin.

ennedy, P. (1989) The Rise and Fall of the Great Powers. London: Fontana Press.

epler, J. (1605) Letter to D. Fabricius, quoted in J. Banville (1981) Kepler. London: Minerva.

epler, J. (1610) Letter to Dr. J. Brengger, quoted in J. Banville (1981) Kepler. London: Minerva.

ershaw, I. (1991) Hitler. Profiles in Power. London: Longman.

estenberg, J. S. (1988) Preface, in M. S. Bergmann, M. E. Jucovy and J. S. Kestenberg (ed.), Kinder der Opfer, Kinder der Täter. Frankfurt am Main: Fischer.

leist, H. von: (1810) Über das Marionettentheater. Leipzig: Insel.

ehmann, A. (1986) Gefangenschaft und Heimkehr. München: Beck.

Lehndorff, H. Graf von (1961) Ostpreussisches Tagebuch. München: Biederstein.

Lessing, H. (ed.) (1984) Kriegskinder. Frankfurt am Main: Extrabuch Verlag.

Lewicki, P., Hill, T. and Czyzewska, M. (1992) Nonconscious acquisition of information. American Psychologist, 47 (6): 796–801.

Lipp, C. (ed.) (1992) Kindheit und Krieg. Frankfurt am Main: Fischer.

Lister-Ford, C. and Pokorny, M. (1994) Individual adult psychotherapy, in P. Clarkson and M. Pokorny (ed.), The Handbook of Psychotherapy. London: Routledge.

Luria, A. R. (1972) The Man with a Shattered World. Cambridge: Harvard University Press.

MacDonald, J. (1986) Great Battles of World War II. London: Joseph.

Main, M., Kaplan, N. and Cassidy, J. (1985) Security in infancy, childhood and adulthood: a move to the level of representation, in I. Bretherton and E. Waters (ed.) Growing Points of Attachment Theory and Research. Chicago: University of Chicago Press.

Marton, F., Fensham, P. and Chaiklin, P. (1994) A Nobel' s eye view of scientific intuition: discussions with Nobel prize-winners in physics, chemistry and medicine (1970-86). Intl. J. Sci. Educ., 16 (4): 457–473.

Matussek, P. (1961) Die Konzentrationslagerhaft als Belastungssituation. Nervenarzt, 32: 538–542

Mazor, A., Gampel, Y., Enright, R. D. and Orenstein, R. (1990) Holocaust survivors: coping with post-traumatic memories in childhood and 40 years later. Journal of Traumatic Stress, 3 (1): 1–14.

Meter, L. (1996) Letters to Barbara,. Woodstock, NY: Overlook Press.

Meyer, S. und Schulze, E. (1985) Von Liebe sprach damals keiner. München: Beck.

Miljević-Ridjički, R. and Lugomer-Armano, G. (1994) Children's Comprehension of War. Child Abuse Review, 3: 134-144.

Miller, A. (1987) For Your Own Good: Roots of Violence in Child-rearing. London: Virago Press.

Minuchin, S. (1974) Families and Family Therapy. London, Tavistock Publications.

Mitcham Jr, S. W. (1995) Kleist, Field-Marshal Ewald von Kleist, in C. Barnett (ed.), Hitler's Generals. London: Phoenix.

Moser, T. (1996) Dämonische Figuren. Die Wiederkehr des Dritten Reiches in der Psychotherapie. Frankfurt: Suhrkamp.

Mulisch, H. (1986) Das Attentat. Hamburg: Rowohlt.

Müller-Hohagen, J. (1988) Verleugnet, verdrängt, verschwiegen. München: Kösel.

Museum Berlin-Karlshorst (ed.) (1997) Erinnerung an einen Krieg. Berlin: Jovis.

Musil, R. (1952) Der Mann ohne Eigenschaften. Hamburg: Rowohlt. [English Translation: R. Musil (1997) The Man without Qualities. London: Picador].

Musil, R. (1999) Die Verwirrungen des Zöglings Törleß. Hamburg: Rowohlt.

Ninh, Bao (1991) The Sorrow of War. London: Minerva.

Onyango, Ph. (1998) The impact of armed conflict on children. Child Abuse Review, 7: 219-229.

Parkes, M. and Napier, M. (1975) Psychiatric Sequelae of Amputation. Contemporary Psychiatry, British Journal of Psychiatry. Ashford: Headley and Brothers.

Pincus, L. and Dare, C. (1978) Secrets in the Family. London: Faber & Faber.

Proust, M. (1954) Du Coté de chez Swan. A la Recherche du Temps perdu. Paris: Gallimard.

Pynoos, R. S., Steinberg, A. M. and Piacentini, J. C. (1999) A developmental psychopathology model of childhood traumatic stress and intersection with anxiety disorders. Biological Psychiatry, 46: 1542–1555.

Ramachandran, V. S. and Blakeslee, S. (1998) Phantoms in the Brain. London: Fourth Estate.

Rauschnigg, H. (ed.) (1985) Das Jahr '45 in Dichtung und Bericht. München: Heyne.

Rees, L. (1999) War of the Century. London: BBC Worldwide.

Remarque, E. M. (1929) All Quiet on the Western Front. London: G. P. Putnam's.

Richter, M. (ed.) (1993) Writers on World War II. London: Vintage.

Rilke, R. M. (1920a) Letter to Leopold von Schlözer from January 1st, 1920, in H. E. Holthusen (1958) Rainer Maria Rilke. Hamburg: Rowohlt.

Rilke, R. M. (1920b) Letter to Generalmajor von Sedlakowitz from December 9th, 1920, in H. E. Holthusen (1958) Rainer Maria Rilke. Hamburg: Rowohlt.

Rilke, R. M. (1997) Die Gedichte. Frankfurt am Main: Insel.

Robinson, S., Rapoport-Bar-Sever, M. and Rapaport, J. (1994) The present state of people who survived the Holocaust as children. Acta Psychiatr. Scand. 89: 242–245.

Rosen, M. (ed.) (1994) The Penguin Book of Childhood. London: Penguin.

Rouaud, J. (1998) Fields of Glory. London: Harvill Press.

Sack, W. H., Clark, G., Chanrithy, H., Dickason, D., Goff, B., Lanham, K. and Kinzie D. (1993) A 6-year follow-up study of Cambodian refugee adolescents traumatized a children. Journal of the American Academy of Child and Adolescent Psychiatry, 32 (2) 431–437.

Sacks, O. (1985) The Man Who Mistook His Wife for a Hat. New York: Alfred A. Knopf.

Sadavoy, J. (1996) Survivors. A review of the late-life effects of prior psychological trauma. The American Journal of Geriatric Psychiatry, 5 (4): 287–301.

Sawin, M. (1998) Das Mitfühlende Objektiv. Kriegsphotographie 1941–1945. Berlin: Elefanten Press.

Schooler, J. W., Ohlsson, S. and Brooks, K. (1993) Thoughts beyond words: when language overshadows insight. Journal of Experimental Psychology: General 122 (2): 166–183.

Segrè, E. (1980) From X-rays to Quarks. Modern Physicists and their Discoveries. New York: W. H. Fremann & Co.

Sereny, G. (2000) The German Trauma. Experiences and Reflections 1938–2000. London: Allen Lane

Shaffer, R. (1977) Mothering. London: Fontana Paperbacks.

Shay, J. (1994) Achilles in Vietnam. Combat Trauma and the Undoing of Character. New York: Touchstone.

Shepard, R. N. (1978) Externalisation of mental images and the act of creation, in B. S. Zandawa and W. E. Lottman (ed.), Visual Learning, Thinking and Communication. New York: Academic Press.

Singh, S. (1997) Fermat's Last Theorem. The Story of a Riddle that Confounded the World's Greatest Minds for 358 Years. London: Fourth Estate.

Slim, W. J. (1986) Defeat into Victory. London: Papermac.

Smith. P. A. (1988) Psychological Effects of War on Children in Bosnia. Thesis for the degree of Doctor of Philosophy, The Institute of Psychiatry, London.

Snow, C. P. (1995) Discovering the Nucleus, in Carey, J. (ed.), The Faber Book of Science. London: Faber & Faber.

teele, J. (1995) Secret scars of families at war. London: The Guardian, 26th August, p. 25.

zpilman, W. (1999) The Pianist. The Extraordinary Story of One Man's Survival in Warsaw, 1939–45. London: Victor Gollancz.

aylor, C. E. (1998) How care for childhood psychological trauma in wartime may contribute to peace. International Review of Psychiatry 10: 175–178.

hamer, H. U. (1986) Verführung und Gewalt. Die Deutschen und ihre Nation. Deutschland 1933–1945. Berlin: Siedler.

he Raphael Lemkin Centenary Conference, 18th October 2000. Announced by the Leo Kuper Foundation (personal communication).

NICEF (1996) State of the World's Children, UN. New York: Oxford University Press.

assiltchikov, Marie 'Missie' (1985) The Berlin Diaries 1940–1945, London: Methuen.

ater ist im Kriege (published at the time of the First World War). Herausgegeben von der Kriegskinderspende deutscher Frauen. Berlin: Hillger.

esper, B. (1985) Die Reise. Frankfurt am Main: März bei Zweitausendeins.

Vardi, D. (1992) Memorial Candles. London: Routledge.

Wedgwood, C. V. ([1938]1992) The Thirty Years War. London: Pimlico.

Viborg, S. (1998) Sein Feld war die Welt (Article about Albert Ballin). Frankfurter Allgemeine Zeitung, No. 259, 7th November, p. 15.

Vickert, J. (1972) Einstein. Hamburg: Rowohlt.

Vicks, B. (1988) No Time To Wave Goodbye. London: Bloomsbury.

Winnicott, D. W. (1971) Playing and Reality. London: Tavistock Publications.

Wulffen, Barbara von (1989) Urnen voll Honig. Frankfurt am Main: Fischer.

ule, W., Perrin, S. and Smith, P. (1999) Post-traumatic stress reactions in children and adolescents, in W. Yule (ed.), Post-Traumatic Stress Disorders: Concepts and Therapy. Chichester: John Wiley & Sons.

ABOUT THE AUTHOR

Dr Peter Heinl MD MRCPsych

Psychiatrist, Psychotherapist and Family Therapist.

Medical studies at the Universities of Heidelberg, Montpellier (Scholarship from the University of Heidelberg), Bochum, Hamburg and Freiburg.

Research work in the laboratories of Professor Dr Dr J. C. Rüegg, Institute of Zellphysiologie, University of Bochum, and of the Nobel Prize Winner Professor Sir Andrew Huxley OM PRS at University College, London.

MD with Magna cum laude and Research Fellowship from the German Academic Exchange Service (DAAD).

Postgraduate Training in Psychiatry and Psychotherapy at the Maudsley Postgraduate Teaching Hospital and Sheldon Fellow of the Advanced Family Therapy Course at the Tavistock Clinic, London.

Member of the Royal College of Psychiatrists (RCPsych).

International Fellow of the American Psychiatric Association (APA).

Member of the Deutsches Kollegium für Psychosomatische Medizin (DKPM).

Patron of the Children-in-War Memorial Day Project.

Member of the Scientific Committee Holocaust Centrum Austria.

Author of numerous innovative publications in the fields of Physiology, Psychiatry, Psychotherapy and Family Therapy, Psychosomatics and Psychotraumatology.

BOOKS WRITTEN AND EDITED
BY THE AUTHOR

UND WIEDER

BLÜHEN DIE ROSEN

Mein Leben nach dem Schlaganfall

Heinl, H.: Thinkaeon, London, 2014 (New edition).

Available as book and ebook via Amazon

Peter Heinl

>Maikäfer flieg, dein Vater ist im Krieg ...‹

Seelische Wunden aus der Kriegskindheit

"MAIKÄFER FLIEG, DEIN VATER
IST IM KRIEG ... "
Seelische Wunden aus der
Kriegskindheit
Heinl, P.: Kösel, München, 1994
(8th edition).

Reviews on www.Amazon.de

Peter Heinl

»MAIKÄFER FLIEG, DEIN VATER IST IM KRIEG«

SEELISCHE WUNDEN AUS DER KRIEGSKINDHEIT

Thinkaeon

New edition

"MAIKÄFER FLIEG, DEIN VATER
IST IM KRIEG ... "
Seelische Wunden aus der
Kriegskindheit
Heinl, P.: Thinkaeon, London, 2014

*Available as book and ebook via Amazon.
Reviews on www.Amazon.de*

**KÖRPERSCHMERZ-
SEELENSCHMERZ**
Die Psychosomatik des
Bewegungssystems
Ein Leitfaden

Heinl, H. und Heinl. P.: Kösel, München 2004
(6th edition).

New edition

**KÖRPERSCHMERZ-
SEELENSCHMERZ**
Die Psychosomatik des
Bewegungssystems
Ein Leitfaden

Heinl, H. und Heinl. P.: Thinkaeon, London, 2015

Available as book and ebook via Amazon.
Reviews on www.Amazon.de

219

Recently published

**LICHT IN DEN OZEAN
DES UNBEWUSSTEN**
Vom intuitiven Denken zur Intuitiven
Diagnostik
Ein Leitfaden in den Denkraum

Heinl, P.: Thinkaeon, London, 2014.

*Available as book and ebook via Amazon.
Reviews on www.Amazon.de*

The impending alarm of war is forcing me to work intensely,
for the days are numbered

Kazimir Malevich, 1915

INDEX

space-time transformations 162–165; symbolism in 61, 64, 72, 163; catalysing mental operations 164–165; catalysing understanding 165; development of 26; effect of 60, 73, 162–165; effects on early traumatic experiences 164; identification in 63–64; time dimension in 72–73

Ohlsson, S. (in Schooler *et al*) 174

Onyango, Ph. 182, 183, 211

open mind 151

Orenstein, R. (in Mazor *et al*) 187

orphans 78; emotional 109

P

pacifists 106, 195

panic attacks 117

paranormal abilities, and intuition 30, 150, 161, 172

parents, age of exposure to war 130; and intuition 133; loss of both 78; mental breakdown 24, 47; misperceiving trauma 140; own childhood 133; relationship between 73, 156, 168, 174, 198; role difficulty 117; war-traumatised 109

peace, longing for 118; trauma continuing into 111–112, 119

perception, accuracy of 154; by professional 29, 42, 132, 135; and child development 133–134; child's 57, 132–133; differentiated from thinking 153; distortion of mother's 189; shift in 104, *see also* communication; intuitive perception; perceptual thinking; and intuitive thinking

perceptual thinking 148–153, *see also* intuitive perception; and intuitive thinking

Perrin, S. (in Yule *et al*) 115, 183

personal development 55–56

Phantoms in the Brain (Ramachandran and Blakeslee) 157

pharmacological treatment 35–36

photographs, trauma evident in 116, 125; use of in therapy 33–34, 127, 156

physical illness 24, 40–41, 81

Piacentini, J. C. (in Pynoos *et al*) 115

Planck, M. 96, 173

play, need for 95

Poincaré, H. 166

polytrauma 101, 103

post-traumatic stress disorder (PTSD) 119, 181

practice, advice on 123–213

pregnancy, depression during 74

prevention, of war 191–213

prisoners of war 36, 47, 52, 94, 107, 108, 128, 129, 130, 131, 135

psychiatrists, sanity of 32, 43–44

psychiatry, child, *see also* child psychiatry

psychosomatic illness 124, 188

psychotherapy 34–35; and intuition 169; and irrational thinking 45–46

PTSD (post-traumatic stress disorder) 119, 181

Pynoos, R. S. 115

Q

questioning, children directly 183; mother 33, 74, 155; in therapy 25, 51, 60, *see also* clinical interview; witnesses, contacting

R

rage 100–101

Ramachandran, V. S. 157

Ramanujan, S. 167–169

Rapaport, J. (in Robinson *et al*) 188

rape 24, 98, 99, 108, 130

rationality 28, 31, 41, 47, 53, 54, 57, 61, 65, 86, 151, 152, 164, 165, 166, 172, *see also* logic

reality, false interpretation of 140; perceiving child's 56, 132–133

Made in the USA
Charleston, SC
23 July 2015